D1482261

With SCALPEL and the SWORD

WITH SCALPEL AND THE SWORD
Copyright © 1997 ABWE Publishing
Harrisburg, PA 17105

Library of Congress cataloging-in-publication data (Application Pending)
Nelson, Lincoln D., 1923 -
    With Scalpel and the Sword: An American Doctor's Odyssey in the Philippines
    Autobiographical, Non-Fiction
    ISBN 1-888796-12-X (Trade Paper)

All rights reserved. No portion of this book may be reproduced in any form without
the written permission of the publisher.

Printed in the United States of America.

Unless otherwise noted, all scriptural quotations are taken from the King James
Version of the Bible.

DEDICATION

This book is dedicated to the most important people in my life:

my wife
LENORE
who has shared the experiences found within these pages and much, much more;

and our five children who were born into a unique band called MK's (Missionary Kids)
LINDA, DAVID, SANDI, MIKE & SHIRLEY
Missionary life would have been impossible without their willingness to share in the lifestyle it demands, and to make invaluable contributions in reaching the goal set before us: to exalt Jesus Christ by placing our talents and energies in His capable hands.

"Who can find a virtuous woman? for her price is far above rubies" (Proverbs 31:10).

"Lo, children are an heritage of the Lord: and the fruit of the womb is his reward.
As arrows are in the hand of a mighty man; so are children of the youth. Happy is the man that hath his quiver full of them: they shall not be ashamed..." (Psalms 127:3-5).

ACKNOWLEDGMENTS

Quite often during our 40 years with the Association of Baptists for World Evangelism, Inc. (ABWE), friends requested that we write down the experiences we shared with them.

For accuracy in recalling details, we appreciate the letters our parents, now in heaven, saved during the years we spent in foreign lands. At our age we needed all the documentation we could find.

Lenore spent hours editing the final draft, and our daughter Sandi Blanchard scanned the manuscript for punctuation and general readability.

We are especially grateful to Dr. J. Sidlow Baxter who contributed valuable insight into the meaning of God creating man "*in His image.*"

Special thanks to close friend and colleague Dr. Darwin Holian who gave his time and expertise on the computer. His ability to convert a PC version of the text into a suitable publishing format was nothing short of amazing.

ABWE Director of Publications, Jeannie Lockerbie Stephenson, was most helpful in bringing together loose ends to finalize the project.

We are indebted to Fred Meise, talented artist and personal friend, for painting a cover design for the book.

To supporting churches and friends who have backed this ministry with prayer and finances, we can only say a hearty "Thank you!"

FOREWORD

Never did I commend a book more gladly than this one. It is not only a book; it is a revelation. It draws aside a curtain and unveils a stage alive with characters and doings little known or realized by most of us. We might almost call it a new Acts of the Apostles. Just as truly today as in the apostolic first century A.D. we see their twentieth century successors, serving, preaching, healing, suffering, persevering, weeping amid frustrations, rejoicing in victories. Souls are still being saved. Trophies are still being won. The Gospel is being preached "in all the world," in lands of which most of us in America know all too little.

This book makes no attempt at capturing our attention by over-coloring the narrative, nor by any other artificiality. It is all fact with no mixture of fiction; which makes it all the more impressive.

As for the author, Dr. & Mrs. Lincoln Nelson are gifted, widely known and much loved veterans of the "holy war" for Christ. They have brought many "out of darkness into His marvelous light," have navigated rough seas, conquered rugged mountains, healed many bodies and souls, and they can say with Paul, "I bear in my body the brands of the Lord Jesus."

So now to their story.

J. Sidlow Baxter, Th.D., D.D.
Santa Barbara, California

TABLE OF CONTENTS

ANECDOTES of a
MEDICAL MISSIONARY

The telegram was not unexpected. Our business manager in the Manila office of ABWE (the Association of Baptists for World Evangelism) had been advised that we might be getting notice from my brother Jim that our father's health was failing. So when Jim phoned Manila, manager Don Love sent an inter-island telegram: PHONE BROTHER ASAP (DON).

The telegram arrived the next day in the small town of Hilongos, our base of operations in Leyte, one of the 7000 islands of the Philippines. Leyte was made famous by the return of the American forces under General MacArthur's command in World War II. The landing site was on the east coast of Leyte near the capital of Tacloban. Hilongos is about 50 miles to the west on the coastline. Another 60 miles due west across the Philippine Sea is Cebu City, second largest urban center in the Republic of the Philippines.

The morning after receiving the telegram, missionary pilot Kevin Donaldson cranked up the Cessna-180 to fly my wife Lenore to Cebu City and the nearest reliable phone for international calls. The best time to place the call was about 10:00 a.m. Because of the time difference, it would be 7:00 p.m. in Santa Barbara, California. I stayed behind with hospital duties.

The call went through relatively quickly. Jim was relieved that we had phoned. He told of Dad's deterioration after a fall in his home where he lived alone since our mother's death three years before. Although he had no broken bones, Dad had been hospitalized for severe bruises and a mild concussion. His doctors planned to release him soon but he would need constant care. Jim and his wife Betty could hire temporary nursing care in the home. But then what? Of

1

we two siblings, who could handle it better?

As medical people nearing retirement, Lenore and I felt this was God's plan for us, and Lenore told Jim our decision. We would wind up our term with the end-of-the-year hospital board and committee meetings. A target date for our departure from the Philippines was set for the end of February, 1987, three months hence.

The reunion with family in Santa Barbara was a happy occasion. Except for memory problems common to the aged, Dad was quite well oriented. We had to move into his condominium and live with him so as not to confuse him with less familiar quarters. It was a learning experience: on-the-job training in geriatrics.

We had to search our own hearts and relationships. What about priorities? What was happening to our commitment to a medical mission ministry in the Philippines or one of the other hospital outreaches of ABWE worldwide? We asked these questions and more of ABWE's president, Wendell Kempton. His reply was thoughtful: "We look at your present status as a special medical furlough. Complete your full year at home. Your primary responsibility *at this time* is to your father."

His words brought to mind a passage of scripture found in the opening verses of the third chapter of the book of Ecclesiastes which applied to our question of priorities: "There is an appointed time for everything ... a time to give birth, and a time to die ... *a time to love and a time to hate.*"

The year passed quickly. Father's health improved remarkably, but he still needed constant companionship. We had promised him we'd stay with him until he was called to heaven. This conviction had come to us as we confronted Christ's own statement:

> For God commanded, saying, Honor thy father and mother:
> ...But ye say, Whosoever shall say to his father or his mother, It is a gift by whatsoever thou mightest be profited by me; And honor not his father or his mother, he shall be free. Thus have ye made the commandment of God of none effect by your tradition. Ye hypocrites...
> (Matthew 15:4-7).

Later the apostle Paul wrote in 1 Timothy 5:8,

> If any provide not for his own, and specially for those of
> his own house, he hath denied the faith, and is worse than
> an infidel.

Yet these quotations have to be balanced against Jesus' other words of equal weight:

> If any man come to me, and hate not his father, and mother,
> and wife, and children, and brethren, and sisters, yea, and
> his own life also, he cannot be my disciple (Luke 14:26).

One of the deciding factors had to do with the realization that the word "hate" in these verses has reference to the assignment of priorities. Are we able to give Christ first place in this change of location and type of work? We made up our minds. We *can*, and we *must*!

"But what about accountability to the faithful supporters of ABWE medical missions over these past 35 years or more?" we asked ourselves.

As at least a partial response, this collection of anecdotes is being written. Some of the donors and prayer partners of this ministry will realize they have been just as much a part of the medical-missions team as we who were privileged to go down to the battle, bearing the **SWORD** (the holy Scriptures) and the **SCALPEL** (the surgeon's knife) to address the needs of suffering people. Certainly in heaven we will share alike, as is recorded in 1 Samuel 30:24.

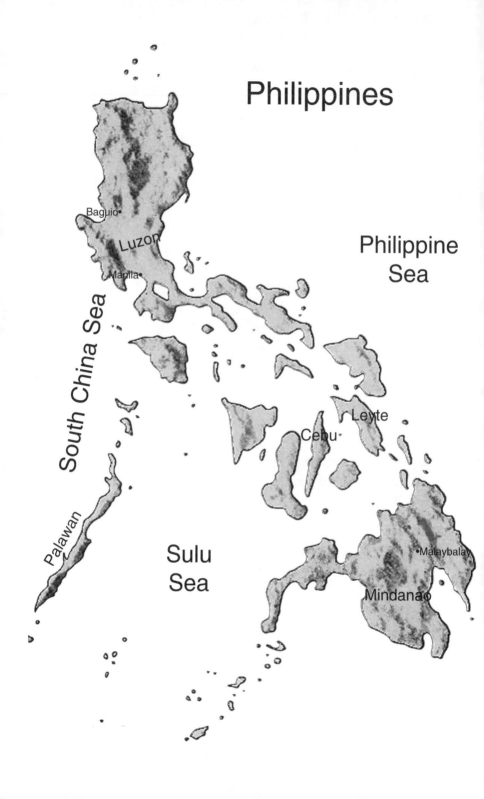

1
PIGS IS PIGS

The day dawned as a usual Sunday in the Philippines: roosters crowing, dogs barking, church bells ringing. A few fleecy clouds were building up over the mountain ranges that rise from the 2,000 foot plateau in central Mindanao, the nation's southernmost island. Most days began this way. Rains often fell in the afternoons and evenings, but mornings were usually bright and sunny.

As was our custom, we planned to visit one of the churches in the area. There were about 20 churches in the fellowship of the Bukidnon Association of Baptist Churches (BABC)[1] at the time. We enjoyed a standing invitation to worship in whichever one we chose, depending on our schedule. Whether we had a prior invitation or not, I usually was asked to preach, so I always carried the outline of a message or two in my Cebuano Visayan Bible — forearmed is a good policy.

In the southern Philippines where we lived during our early years as ABWE missionaries, the major dialects are in the Visayan language group. Among these, the Cebuano branch is dominant. I was just getting sufficiently confident with the language to preach in it, though not without blunders. My outlines were in English with a column of important vocabulary words for the Cebuano rendition. Still, it required a most hospitable and long-suffering congregation to sit through those first sermons. The informality helped. It wasn't unusual for someone to prompt me if I hesitated over a phrase.

On this Sunday we were heading south on Sayre Highway, the main road running from Cagayan de Oro City on the northern coast of Mindanao to the southern coastal city of Davao. The road ran

[1] Appendix C

through our town, Malaybalay, the capital of Bukidnon province. It wasn't paved at that time except for short stretches through major towns and some villages. Sayre was the U.S. army engineer who supervised the reconstruction of this highway during the closing years of World War II when the American forces returned to the Philippines to drive out the Japanese war machine.

This highway, like the many others constructed by the army, crossed innumerable rivers and streams over single-lane bridges of angle-iron framework and plank flooring. We called them "Bailey bridges," after the architect, I assume. They were mechanically sound, some still in active use to this day.

The roads were gravel and the bridges single lane. As we drove out of town, the first bridge was thoroughly obstructed by a passenger bus. Please don't picture a "Greyhound" in your mind. Rather, consider something on the order of a large truck with the bed enclosed in a frame structure, having windows and roofed over with galvanized iron sheet metal. For seats, two rows of wooden benches were anchored to the floor. The width of each bench could accommodate the proportions of three average Filipinos but seemed uncomfortably cramped to the average Caucasian hip measurements, if the conductor insisted on full occupancy. And he usually did! We assumed the delay was the result of some mechanical failure at a most inconvenient site for those who had hoped to traverse that bridge.

The Filipino believes in fate, and fate has its privileges. If a truck breaks down in the middle of a road, or on a bridge, obviously *fate* assigned that space to the unfortunate victim and he may occupy that space until proper repairs enable him to resume his journey. If others are inconvenienced thereby, *fate* says, "Too bad!" The fact that the driver may leave large boulders in the road where they had been used to block his wheels to prevent rolling also seems to be an accepted by-product of *fate* — a memorial of the incident.

We stopped. To our surprise, off the bus jumped someone we recognized, Dick Elkins, of the Wycliffe Bible Translators. He and his wife Betty were reducing into writing the language of a primitive Manobo tribe living in the mountains of central Mindanao. He told us why the bus had stopped. He had recognized our jeep approaching from a distance and persuaded the driver to stop on the bridge so that he would have no trouble intercepting us. The driver agreed. Dick joined us and the bus went on its way.

"I've got a problem," Dick explained. "There has been an accident. One of the Manobo hunters has been gored by a wild boar, and the man is in bad shape. We couldn't carry him down from his mountain village because the trail is too difficult, and the relatives fear he'd die on the way. That would be a greater disaster than having him die at home. I did what I could and then told them I'd go for medical help. That was about five hours ago."

We all went back to the mission house to collect our medical kit used in emergencies and to change into proper clothes for the work ahead. Lenore and our two kids, Linda (age three) and David (age two), shifted their church attendance to the nearby chapel. Dick and I headed the Jeep station wagon south toward Kibawe, the closest village on the highway to the injured man's settlement. The 50-mile (80 kilometer) drive took four hours.

One of the Filipino evangelists, Brother Max, who was fluent in the dialect of these Manobos, joined us when we got to Kibawe. Like many Filipinos, he could speak several Filipino languages as well as English. He also had the heart to help people who were suffering, and I never saw him without a smile on his face. He genuinely loved God and effectively communicated the truths in scripture to even the least schooled of tribesmen. He had "walked in their shoes"— or, in their case, "thongs."

We parked the Jeep in the yard of a friend. The remainder of the journey required hiking along jungle trails leading into the mountains. Manobo guides led the way, carrying our supplies. For an hour we tried to keep up with them. We were glad when they finally paused by a waterfall to give us a break. They seemed impatient, but while we rested these guides intently studied the depths of the pool below the falls.

"He's still alive!" they confided. Relief was evidenced by their more relaxed demeanor.

"Who told them that?" I asked the evangelist.

"They didn't see his sleeping mat on the floor of the pool," was his explanation. He told of a superstition among Manobos in that area: when one of their tribesmen dies, the spirits carry his mat to the bottom of the pool. Since it wasn't there, he must be alive! Simple. So we continued on. "One more hill," they assured us, though it looked like a mountain to me. More mud. More slipping and sliding. I was glad someone else was carrying my case of surgical instruments and supplies.

Dogs announced our arrival. God must love dogs; He has allowed so many of them to survive in every country we've visited. They even attend church services. Some are more consistent in church attendance than the people who should be there. Nobody pays attention to them — unless there's a dog fight down the center aisle. This remote village of thatched roof huts had plenty of dogs. They seemed to slink away from us, but they were even in the house where we were taken to see the injured man. So were all of his neighbors and relatives. One saving feature of the style of house they lived in was that one wall was left open for light and ventilation. The wall was made of woven bamboo, the roof of thatch. The floor made of rattan felt springy to our feet when we walked across it to see the victim of the goring who lay in the most remote corner.

His wound had been bound up with a cloth of some sort. It wasn't a diaper, to be sure. Tribal babies didn't wear them. But there was a resemblance, in more ways than one. To evaluate his condition more carefully, I asked if the patient could be lifted onto the one table which constituted the sole piece of furniture in the room. That required disturbing the dog which was on it. After the table had been moved to better lighting, and the patient had been positioned upon it, I was able to begin.

Relatives and other curious bystanders crowded into the room. After removing the wrappings, I prepared to hear a sucking sound from the wound in his chest. Surprise! No such noise. The reason was soon obvious. Jungle first-aid had successfully plugged the opening into the chest cavity: guava leaves! A big wad of them.

There is indeed merit in such treatment. The crushed guava leaf has an astringent property which stops bleeding, and its moistness effectively blocks any escape or entrance of air.

For this reason, the partially collapsed lung beneath had begun to expand as nature sealed some of its surface laceration. The delay in reaching him had not been critical. But I do wish they wouldn't chew the leaves before pressing them into wounds!

I began the more delicate work. Of course I had to anesthetize the patient before I could proceed with cleaning and suturing the wound.

"Dick," I mumbled, "I'll need another pair of hands here. Have you ever helped with surgery before?"

"That wasn't in my linguistic curriculum!" he replied. But he was willing to learn. I showed him how to improvise an instrument stand by turning an empty, heavy-duty grain basket upside down beside us. Then, after we had opened our sterile supplies, he followed me in the technique of putting on surgeons' gloves. The evangelist became our lamp-stand, holding a flashlight over our heads and, usually, directing the light into the wound.

The local anesthetic comes in 20 milliliter vials. I drew one vial into a large syringe, attached a three-inch needle, held it up to flush out the bubble of air. The crowded room suddenly emptied, except for the operating team.

From then on the procedure went smoothly. I cleared away the debris, thoroughly cleaned the wound and closed with layers of suture. After the chest was closed, I withdrew most of the air trapped in the chest cavity through a large syringe. We didn't dare leave a chest tube in place to drain off any further collection of fluid or air as is usually done. Who would follow up on its care? We injected a generous dose of penicillin intramuscularly and bandaged the chest with a sterile dressing. We asked the Lord to spare his life, then returned him to his mat in the corner.

By the time we had cleaned up the instruments and packed things into the carrying cases, the crowd was back. This time we saw happy faces and evident confidence in a good outcome for their loved one.

Then we learned how our patient had been injured.

He had been hunting for wild boar, a succulent meat. Some hunters improvise small bombs encased in ping-pong balls and place them in a field where the boars are likely to feed. One bite and they lose their heads. But this hunter had used a spear with a detachable steel head. When this is plunged into the boar, it pulls free except for a short length of rope that attaches the barbed head to the shaft. When the injured boar tries to escape, the rope drags the shaft through the underbrush, eventually snagging a bush. The finishing blows put meat on the table.

But pigs are unpredictable. This wounded one turned on the hunter and had time to lunge at him, ripping open his chest with a sharp tusk. As the saying goes, "Pigs is pigs." It's their nature to be quick, vicious, and ill-tempered, especially with a spear caught in their flesh.

Before we left, we asked the villagers if we might tell them a story. Not about pigs, about snakes. Oh yes, they love to hear stories. Their primitive lifestyle is built around superstition and fear. They engage in animistic rituals which endeavor to appease the spirit world. These rituals often include a blood sacrifice, usually using a chicken. A village priest officiates, chanting incantations appropriate to the occasion.

These people had not heard of a God of creation who loved them. They did not know that this creator God had provided a way for mankind to worship Him and to please Him. They had not heard that God had provided another blood sacrifice, Jesus Christ, to cure the wound of the soul resulting from the sickness called sin.

That's where the snake story fit in. As our omniscient God alone might do, He had prepared Dick for this hour. In his bag Dick had brought along an early draft of his translation of a story in the Bible about the people of God called the Hebrews. They had been miraculously delivered from slavery in Egypt. But while crossing the desert to the land God was providing for them, they had grumbled, complained and in general rebelled against God. As punishment, God had sent poisonous snakes into their camp. The people who were bitten died, until God provided a way of salvation for them.

Their leader, Moses, was ordered to make a snake out of brass and lift it up on a pole. Those who trusted God's way of deliverance by looking at that serpent were spared. Those who tried other ways of deliverance died.

Brother Max read this story from the paper Dick handed him. Words in Manobo were coming from that paper to the ears of those who were in that house. *God was speaking Manobo!*

That introduction was an opening similar to that which was given to Philip in Acts 8:35, which reads, "... and began at the same scripture, and preached unto him *Jesus*."

Today there are several churches among the Manobo tribes people. The last time I saw that injured Manobo he was standing in a crowd at the edge of the highway as we had a special outdoor gospel meeting. He lifted his shirt to point out the well-healed scar on his chest. Otherwise, I might not have recognized him at all.

Do you wonder that a news item in the local paper on June 10, 1988 captured my attention when the headlines blared: "$16 MILLION F-16 JET DESTROYED AFTER HITTING 2 PIGS ON RUNWAY" (*Santa Barbara New Press*, June 10, 1988).

Apparently, whether in the jungles of the Philippines or on the concrete runways of the Jacksonville International Airport, "PIGS IS PIGS"!

2

MAKING PATHS STRAIGHT

"Trust in the Lord with all thine heart
and lean not unto thine own understanding.
In all thy ways acknowledge Him, and He shall direct thy paths"
(Proverbs 3:5,6).

I had no idea what a medical missionary was until I heard one speak at a youth camp I attended the summer before I entered the sixth grade. From then on, I knew what I wanted to be: a physician like Doctor Brown. He had worked in Africa for many years, though I cannot recall the details. He treated sick people and told them about Jesus.

That was in 1935. The definition of a medical missionary has taken on a fuller meaning since then. For one thing he is a medically trained and licensed professional. In my case that meant majoring in a premedical program at Wheaton College in Illinois. In my sophomore year, World War II broke out. President Franklin D. Roosevelt announced the entrance of the USA into the war on a radio news-break on December 7, 1941, when the Japanese bombed U.S. ships in Pearl Harbor. Immediately, everyone's life took on a new dimension. Every college student was asking, "Now what?"

I'll never forget Dr. V. R. Edman, president of Wheaton College, counseling us, "It's always too soon to quit!" We were advised to continue our college work until specifically involved in the war effort. For those of us in the premedical program, options opened. We could finish our college course if we enlisted in a branch of the military. The V-12 program of the U.S. Navy appealed to me, so I signed up.

13

I wrote my parents about that decision. We were a close-knit family. Mother and Dad were very supportive of their two sons. My brother Jim was older than I by four years and married to his college sweetheart, Betty. Jim was in Dallas Theological Seminary studying for church ministry. That pleased Dad, an executive officer of an industry in Maryland, for he was a self-taught Bible scholar and active in his home church.

I also wrote the news to my childhood sweetheart, Lenore Butts, who was attending Baptist Bible Seminary in Johnson City, New York. Our two families had become close friends when we attended the Cazenovia Park Baptist Church in Buffalo, New York. My parents later sold our house in the suburbs to Lenore's family. Little did our parents realize what this real estate transaction might lead to. Each claimed they got the better deal in the bargain. In 1939 the Nelson family moved to Salisbury, Maryland when my father's business moved south. In spite of the geographic separation, Lenore and I kept up a roaring correspondence.

As soon as the prerequisites at Wheaton were completed, I was accepted in medical college at the University of Buffalo in western New York. Classes began in the summer of 1943 and the four-year curriculum was compressed into three years. There were no long summer breaks, only one week off between trimesters. Saturday mornings were devoted to military training and drills at the armory. Male students wore uniforms at all times, settling what to wear when we prepared for classes every day. Furthermore, we were paid to attend medical school and our uniforms were provided. We even received a $50 cash stipend each month for the extras.

A few months after entering medical college I went to Lenore's father, Mike Butts, requesting permission to marry his daughter. He graciously gave his consent. In a few months I had saved enough of my monthly Navy stipend to buy the rings. Late one evening I slipped the one-eighth carat diamond ring onto the fourth finger of her left hand and asked her to be my bride. As fireworks burst in the sky from the nearby Erie County fair grounds, and other invisible tremors filled my chest, Lenore replied in the affirmative.

One more hurdle had to be crossed before setting a date for the wedding. Student nurses were not allowed to marry while in training. Lenore presented her request to the supervising nurse. To our delighted relief, Lenore was the first nursing student permitted to marry while in training as a special wartime concession.

So during the June break between trimesters in 1944, we were married in the First Baptist Church of Hamburg, New York. We considered ourselves rich: the Navy paid married midshipmen an extra $50 a month. Our honeymoon was at nearby Lime Lake, near Machias, the Odosagih Bible Conference site. This was where, in 1935, I had attended the youth camp which set me on the path of becoming a medical missionary.

After the wedding Lenore still had to reside in the nurses' dormitory at her hospital until she graduated, married or not! But I had quarters in a private home only a block away. We both received degrees with honors from professional schools in June 1946. Concurrently, I was commissioned as a Lieutenant (jg) in the Medical Corps Reserve of the U.S. Navy.

The final hurdle in my training was the required internship. The Navy allowed that to be done in either a military or a civilian hospital. I chose the latter and was accepted to enter Hackensack Hospital, Hackensack, New Jersey.

I preceded Lenore by two months since she had a few finishing requirements. This gave me time to find housing next to the hospital. The rent was $52 per month and my stipend was $50/month. So if we were to eat, Lenore had to work, too. When she arrived, she got a job at the same hospital where I was. How good of the Lord to demonstrate His care so practically. We have His promise, "My God shall supply all your needs according to His riches in glory by Christ Jesus" (Philippians 4:19).

We thoroughly enjoyed our time in Hackensack. Not only was the training excellent preparation for the medical board examinations, but we also were introduced to a church where Dr. Harry Leech gave solid Bible teaching. We received both medical experience and spiritual nourishment there. We also developed lasting friendships and reinforced our interest in medical missions.

Of course, the Navy had a claim on our lives for several years. I thought this would be a hindrance to getting into active missionary work, but we soon saw God's hand in the Naval assignments after our year in Hackensack.

The first of these was a six-month hitch on the surgical service of the U.S. Naval Hospital, Philadelphia. As a resident in surgery, I increasingly gained more hands-on experience. Simultaneously, we were able to begin the process of joining the mission agency with which we would work as missionaries after my military requirements were completed.

It happened this way. We had become impressed with the agency in which friends of ours were serving: the Association of Baptists For World Evangelism, Inc., commonly known as ABWE. The headquarters of this mission was in Philadelphia. Soon after our arrival in that city, we contacted the president, Dr. Harold T. Commons. We told him of our interest in the mission and of our military status.

He was most cordial and asked where we were staying. At that time we were sweltering in a one-room utility apartment on the south side of the city. He suggested we consider moving into the beautiful, spacious accommodations of the mission's guest house in Germantown. What a difference that move made. Before long, we were cementing relationships with office personnel and ABWE missionaries passing through, en route to or from their overseas postings.

The month we spent there was an education. We learned what a mission agency does. It does not usurp the responsibility of local churches to send missionaries overseas, nor does a faith mission take on the financial responsibility associated with such enterprises. Rather, a mission agency such as ABWE comes to the aid of local churches by supplying its expertise in helping them accomplish the complex task.

And it *is* complex! The agency screens each candidate through a battery of tests: physical, psychological and theological. Then the candidate attends orientation classes to become acquainted with the mission's principles and practices. A walk-through of the ABWE office apprises the candidate of the immense involvement of behind-the-scenes personnel who take care of the secretarial, financial, and communication department functions.

Administrators help line up speaking engagements for the prospective missionary after his appointment. The treasurer spells out the basic financial support figure required for an appointee before he can leave for the field of his choice. Finally, the "how-to" of getting the necessary documents for the foreign traveler is outlined.

We applied to ABWE to be medical evangelists upon our separation from the Navy. We met with the ABWE Board and were approved for membership in the fall of 1947.

At that time ABWE was assembling a task force of missionaries to enter Dutch New Guinea. It was to be led by Rev. Henry DeVries, a senior missionary who had pioneered the work in the Philippines in the 1930's. Because he had stirred our interest in ABWE when he visited our home church some years before, we had a bond with him and his wife Gladys. The mission suggested we consider joining that team. We felt it was the Lord's direction for us, and we accepted.

In January, 1948 I received the next set of orders: report to the Naval Air Station in Anacostia, Maryland. This tour of duty provided me with the medical training needed for working with pilots of Naval aircraft, the first step in becoming a Flight Surgeon.

The introduction to aviation whetted my appetite to eventually become a pilot myself. From this strategic one-year experience I was prepared for the overseas assignment required of qualified medical officers. The Lord saw to it that the orders read: "REPORT TO THE USN STATION, SUBIC BAY, PHILIPPINES..." followed by the time, date and other particulars. We were on our way to the mission field under the auspices of the U.S. government! Can anyone deny that God was directing our steps?

We wrote a letter to friends who were interested in our progress toward missionary work. Excerpts from that letter dated May 1949 stated:

"We were considering the possibility of work on the ABWE field in Dutch New Guinea, or that group of islands to the northwest of there — the Philippines. Then along came what seems to us to be God's answer, for in December of 1948 the Navy Bureau of Medicine informed me that a vacancy would be coming up soon for dispensary duty at Subic Bay in the Philippines and that I could have the job by applying for it and agreeing to stay in the Navy until July 1950. Lenore would be able to go along, our household effects and car would all be shipped there at government expense, and I could have 18 months of experience with tropical medicine among the Filipinos.

"So we left Washington, D.C. the last week of January 1949 and boarded the *USAT General Buckner* on March 8 at San Francisco — Manila bound!"

We had gone through an emotion-packed departure aboard the military transport ship in March 1949. Relatives saw us off. Paper streamers snapped as the ship eased away from the pier, breaking the fragile ties held by loved ones being left behind. A Navy band played, "Now is the Hour," as we watched the skyline of San Francisco slowly recede while the ship slipped beneath the Golden Gate Bridge into the open Pacific.

There were few dry eyes among the passengers: men in uniform leaving their families; a few wives and children en route to join their husbands overseas. Lenore and I were the only married couple aboard, as far as we could determine.

That wasn't exactly the way the commanding officer in the Philippines had expected it. Officers had to have assigned quarters for married personnel before sending for their wives. Getting such quarters required several months of waiting for a vacancy. However, the fact that I had received orders while in the D.C. area enabled me to go personally to the Navy department and request permission for Lenore to accompany me. We had to prove that Lenore could live outside the Navy base in the Philippines.

No problem. ABWE personnel in Manila sent an official letter of invitation for her to live with the Hopewell family until Navy quarters became available. So Lenore's name was included in the orders for travel on the transport!

We learned several things on that cruise. Within the first day or two we realized that we didn't have "sea-legs." The first meal in the officers' mess was an exciting new experience. But as the seas got higher, fewer and fewer of the passengers showed up for meals. The few who did come didn't bring their appetites. A couple of the high chairs for the little tots tipped over because of the swells. That about did it for everyone.

We awoke one morning to increasingly rough seas. Lenore rushed to the "head" (Navy terminology for a bathroom) and lost whatever was still in her stomach. I rolled over, expressing my sympathy for her discomfort. After all, she was in the second trimester of her first pregnancy, so it was the expected thing to happen. However, when I sat up on the edge of the bunk to explain the phenomenon to her, it became apparent to me that pregnancy isn't the only cause for morning sickness! I also rushed for a place at the sink.

We found it wise to spend more time on deck where the crisp open air could repress the nausea. Not surprisingly, quite a few were making the crossing, including the ship's doctor who was on his first voyage across the Pacific.

How grateful we all were when we passed the landswells and the Pacific was as tranquil as its name implied. The ship docked in Hawaii for a day. Buses drew alongside and as many as wished to do so had a tour of Oahu. This was our first taste of a tropical paradise. The ship weighed anchor sometime during the night and we awoke to see nothing on the horizon but open seas.

How insignificant we felt, viewing such an expanse of God's handiwork! The Psalmist David must have felt the same when he wrote:

> When I consider thy heavens, the work of thy fingers, the moon and the stars, which thou hast ordained; what is man that thou art mindful of him? ... O Lord our Lord, how

excellent is thy name in all the earth (Psalm 8:3-4,9).

The crossing took nearly three weeks. We enjoyed a special party on board when we crossed the International Date Line in the tropics just a few degrees north of the equator. We saw our first sight of the Philippines as the ship entered the San Bernadino Straits, venue of major sea battles with the Japanese fleet only a few years earlier. Islands on each side were lush and green with coconut groves and jungle.

Luzon on the starboard side, the largest of the seven thousand islands making up the archipelago, proudly displayed the perfect cone of Mount Mayon, a volcano with a wisp of smoke crowning its peak. We slept little that night as we anticipated landing the next morning.

Majestically the ship passed Corregidor, sentinel island at the mouth of Manila Bay. The Bataan Peninsula lay aport. These were now historic sites of battles that had raged in the early 1940's. MacArthur and his staff had transferred to Australia just prior to the surrender of General Wainwright to the Japanese invaders. As we crossed the bay to berth in Manila, we were impressed by the harbor bristling with partially sunken warships and rusted anti-aircraft guns still pointing skyward as though expecting yet another air attack.

Imagine our delight on March 28 when we saw in the waving crowd on the pier, far below our deck, a group of ABWE missionaries waiting for us to disembark: Ed Bomm, the Spahrs, and the Hopewells who had invited Lenore to stay with them. I had a few days to see her comfortably settled before proceeding to the Naval base at Subic Bay. This was Holy Week prior to Easter, 1949. Our missionary friends showed us some of the sights of the city: public buildings in ruins; the former prison camp for American hostages in Santo Tomas University; streets crowded with horse drawn vehicles, Jeepneys (colorful local taxis constructed from metal frames placed on Jeep chassis) and pedestrians.

On Good Friday we visited a beach on which the *flagellantes* enacted the drama of Christ's suffering by beating their own bared backs with whips and thongs till they fell exhausted. Though newspaper reporters applauded these acts of penitence, no approval or merit for such self-abuse is found in scripture. Titus 3:5,6 tells us, Not by works of righteousness which we have done, but according to his mercy he saved us, by the washing of regeneration and renewing of the Holy Ghost; which he shed on us abundantly through Jesus Christ our Savior.

No other sacrifice is acceptable to God than that of His Son Jesus, Who gave His life *once* for all people, for all time. It was evident that we had arrived in a country that was religious but not righteous. Four hundred years of domination by Spain had left the Philippines with ninety percent of its population professing to be Roman Catholic. Yet these citizens of the "only Christian nation in the Orient" were woefully ignorant of the Word of God.

Since saving faith comes through hearing and heeding the Word of God (Romans 10:17), there was an urgent need for preachers of the gospel of Jesus Christ — missionaries! Now I more fully understood the definition of a medical missionary: *one who wields both the scalpel and the Sword:*

For the word of God is quick, and powerful, and sharper than any twoedged sword, piercing even to the dividing asunder of soul and spirit, and of the joints and marrow, and is a discerner of the thoughts and intents of the heart (Hebrews 4:12).

What better place to begin fusing these functions of medical missions than in the U.S. Navy? When I arrived at the Naval Station, Subic Bay, my medical missionary vocation in the Philippines began.

At the same time Lenore was invited to stay with the missionary ladies who were in charge of the ABWE vacation facilities in Baguio City. This was especially welcome since that city is slightly over 4000 feet in elevation and much cooler than Manila. The tropical heat was getting to her, and she was much more comfortable in Baguio. She was also able to meet many missionaries who came for a few weeks of rest. They gave her insights into their ministries, their victories and their set-backs.

Some of those missionaries had survived World War II only by the grace of God, for they had been imprisoned by the Japanese when the country was invaded early in 1942 and the American forces had to withdraw temporarily. They had suffered much. Nevertheless, after their miraculous release by the U.S. troops in 1945, many of them regained sufficient health to return to their beloved adopted land and continue their missionary work. Tough soldiers of the cross!

It was a happy day when orders came from COMNAVPHIL, the Commander of Naval Forces in the Philippines, to transfer to the Naval Air Station, Sangley Point, Cavite. This base, the admiral's headquarters, was much closer to Manila on a peninsula that jutted into Manila Bay, much like a finger pointing at the city from the southwest. The medical officers had been rotated back to the USA and I was to fill the vacancy. The Executive Officer assured me that there would be another doctor or two arriving soon to fill the other slots. But the best news was that we could move into the vacated officers' quarters! It didn't take me long to notify Lenore and make the transfer. We had been in the Philippines only two months.

Our assigned residence was one of the Quonset buildings used by the military for such accommodations. Though many comforts, such as air-conditioning, were lacking, it was our home. Corrugated galvanized iron sheets made up the bulk of the house. These popped and groaned as the heat of the day waxed or waned, causing expansion or contraction of the sheet metal. We got used to it. Among the luxuries was an electric ice-cream maker attached to the deep freeze. We got used to that, too!

It was not hard to get acquainted with our neighbors, officers' families of similar rank. And to Lenore's delight, several of the wives were also in their last trimester of pregnancy. Since I was their obstetrician, we all bonded nicely. Several of these friendships have continued to this day. As it turned out, I was the only doctor on board for nearly a year. My job description required many hats. I was a general specialist, exactly how I would serve for the first ten years as a medical missionary without another doctor to help with the responsibilities.

Unexpectedly, the commanding officer asked me to draw up a floor plan for the construction of the Naval hospital at Sangley Point. The original building had been bombed into oblivion. The decision was to rebuild on the site of the former nurses' dormitory. All that remained of that structure was the cement slab, which could be used as part of the foundation. I was fascinated as I inspected the progress being made each day on the construction of that Naval hospital. After all, it was *my* hospital! Our future missionary career would involve drawing up floor plans for three mission hospitals in the southern part of that same country.

But before we moved into the new facilities, there was plenty of excitement in the old hospital made up of a cluster of Quonset buildings situated at the extreme tip of the peninsula. It was about a mile down the road from our living quarters. The senior medical officer's Jeep was designated for my use since I was the only doctor.

I was also on call for emergencies 24 hours a day, seven days a week. Fortunately, this didn't prove too demanding. At least my memory of night calls seems to center around the obstetrical service. No one has explained to my satisfaction why it is that babies seem to prefer arriving during the night. Storks apparently favor flying after dark. They must enjoy going by IFR (Instrument Flight Rules) navigation.

One delivery stands out above all others in our memories. That was when Lenore went into labor August 6, 1949. We had been looking forward to this blessed event with keen anticipation. Preparations included the usual selection of announcement cards to be mailed when the facts were all in.

Since my findings of a fetal heart rate during the monthly prenatal check-ups were consistent with that of a male, I concluded it would be safe to print on the announcements:
"IT'S JUST WHAT THE DOCTOR ORDERED: A HEALTHY BABY BOY!"
It must be said to my credit that I didn't think it wise to presuppose the weight of the child, too. But it must also be stated here that the prediction of the sex of the child never went into print. Lenore persuaded me to leave a blank to be filled in by pen, "just in case..." And a good thing it was that she prevailed. Linda is hardly a *boy's* name!

August 6 started in the usual way: with the crackle and pop of our Quonset as it welcomed the morning sun. The lovely songs of a variety of birds joined the announcement of the dawn of another bright tropical day. I got up, leaving Lenore to follow at a pace commensurate with her condition. Irregular contractions had made sleeping less sound for her. She needed the few extra winks.

But that day was not to be "as usual." It was a Saturday for one thing. That meant only a half-day at the office for me. Since the section for dependents had no in-patients, the duty nurse returned to her quarters to await possible emergency calls.

Meanwhile, Lenore told me that our missionary friends in Manila, the Bancrofts, had phoned to ask if they could visit us that afternoon. We enjoyed having ABWE friends visit, for it gave them a relaxing change from the city. They could swim in the officers' pool and eat some of the delicacies that civilians lacked or couldn't afford.

Lenore warned them that they might have to get their own supper, however, since she wasn't feeling too well. The Bancrofts were especially close to us since Lenore had lived in their home while attending seminary in New York state. They arrived and off to the pool they went.

It was soon evident that the ill feeling and cramping Lenore had been experiencing were signals of an imminent birth. Neither of us gave her symptoms much heed until one last visit to the bathroom warned her that we didn't have time to loiter. I phoned the nurse to meet us at the hospital right away. Off we roared in the Jeep, with a quick explanation to our guests.

The hospital was unusually quiet. We had arrived ahead of the nurse. I took Lenore straight to the delivery room and told her to disrobe while I did the same in the doctors' dressing room. But the locker with the gowns and scrub suits was locked and I had no key. I was clad only in my "unders" and Lenore by this time was awaiting the modest covering of a sheet in the adjacent room.

Happily the nurse arrived in time to get the sheet and to unlock the cabinet holding my scrub suit. All that remained was to slip on a pair of surgical gloves and welcome Linda Diane into this hectic world.

This tour of duty in the Philippines added dimension to our lives. Since the Navy extended medical care to the officers and enlisted men and their families, I had increasing experience in a general family practice that included Filipinos as well as Americans. We even delivered three babies of missionary wives. Each wife arrived on the station for a visit of a few days. The fact that she went into labor while there forced us to accept her as a patient under the "humanitarian" clause of the Rules and Regulations of Navy hospitals overseas.

Perhaps the most memorable of those deliveries was that of Martha Wray. Her husband, Gordon, was the director of the Doane Baptist Bible Institute (DBBI) in Iloilo City on the island of Panay in central Philippines where ABWE began its work. The Wray family knew of our intention to work with ABWE and wanted to meet us while we were at the Naval station.

So in early June 1950, Gordon and Martha and their two children, Nancy and Philip, packed up and flew two hundred miles north to Manila. ABWE friends in Manila volunteered to keep the Wray children while Gordon and Martha made their way to our home on the Naval base. Ruth Hopewell, also in her last week of pregnancy, accompanied them since I was to be her obstetrician, too.

Their ride on the Navy barge across Manila Bay to Sangley Point was understandably tiring. But Lenore, gifted in hospitality, soon made them as comfortable as possible. In the evenings, we played the table game Sorry for entertainment. Within a few days, Ruth delivered a precious baby girl, and the Hopewells returned to Manila.

Two *weeks* later, we were *still* playing Sorry with Gordon and Martha, much to their dismay. But then the signs we were waiting for began. We hustled Martha over to the hospital's delivery room. Gordon asked if he might be able to observe, and I agreed. He was masked and gowned and assigned to an out-of-the-way place where he could observe the proceedings.

Martha's progress through natural childbirth was faster than anticipated. She gave us no time for pain relievers to take effect.

Little Danny came screaming into the world. While I finished up by ligating the cord, from the corner of the room Gordon blurted out, "Man, that was as easy as falling off a log!"

Lenore and I feared that Gordon's comment might bring to an end that happy marriage. Martha graciously forgave Gordon, but none of us has forgotten that night — nor Gordon's *faux pas*.

3

GETTING STARTED

*"Being confident of this very thing, that he which hath
begun a good work in you will perform it until the day of
Jesus Christ" (Philippians 1:6).*

God had to prepare us for the specific assignment He had in mind
for us. We didn't necessarily know it at the time, but every new or
different experience was a piece of the puzzle which would later
become a picture with God's signature at the bottom.

For we are His workmanship, created in Christ Jesus unto
good works, which God hath before ordained that we
should walk in them (Ephesians 2:10).

Let me give you an example. While we were based at the Naval
Air Station, Sangley Point, Cavite for over a year, we began to realize
that the Philippines might be the country in which we would
eventually serve as missionaries with ABWE. We had kept in touch
with the agency and it was becoming more evident that because of
government restrictions ABWE could not open a work in Dutch New
Guinea in the foreseeable future. Since that was true, we felt that
this experience in the Philippines was another of God's ways of
indicating His choice for us.

I wrote a general letter to friends who were interested in our
progress toward missionary work. Excerpts from that letter dated in
May 1949 stated ...

"Our appointment under the Association of
Baptists for World Evangelism was tentatively for
New Guinea, but that field has not been opened to the

ABWE.

Now the Lord has shown us another evidence of His guidance which has given us further assurance that He wants us to stay in the Philippines as missionaries when the Navy tour is over. While considering how much is needed in the line of hospital supplies for a mission hospital, I learned that the Navy is about to release 60 hospital beds and some other very good equipment that is in excess of the needs of the base. The officer in charge said that I can have first choice at $5 a bed, and as ridiculously low a price for the other supplies.

This should become available within the next month and we will try to get 30 of the adjustable beds along with other supplies and store them here until we are ready. It pays to be the heirs of a King, doesn't it?"

I wondered if now might be the best time to try to get my medical license to practice in the Philippines, rather than waiting until after being released from the Navy. We even considered starting my discharge process so that when this tour of duty was over, we could remain in the Philippines, saving the time and expense of travelling to the States and then back to the Philippines. However in June 1950 that idea was shot down. The Korean War interrupted all plans for early discharge from military service.

Nevertheless in the middle of 1949 I began to make inquiry about the requirements for getting a Philippine medical license. It turned out to be a complicated process. There was the question of reciprocity with the state in which I was already licensed in the USA.

I found out that the word "reciprocity" meant quite a different thing in the two countries involved. In the States, reciprocity meant that a licensed physician could be licensed in another state with similar requirements without even taking another examination. In the Philippines it meant that if the state in which I was licensed allowed Filipino doctors to practice there *without becoming citizens* of the

USA, then I would be allowed to take the examinations for licensure in the Philippines. I began the paperwork, finding out that Maryland, in which I was licensed at the time, did meet this requirement for reciprocity. Not many states did.

Finally the documents were gathered, which was no small matter considering the distance between our countries. I had to make several trips to the office of the Secretary of the Board of Medical Examiners in Manila to get everything in order. At last the dates of the examination in January 1950 were announced and I was allowed to enroll. The written tests would take four days: two sections of two days each, separated by a weekend break.

I completed the first day and arrived for the second. After being seated, I was approached by the examiner and told that there was a notice from the Secretary of the Board that my papers were not yet in order for taking the examinations and I would have to defer completing the tests until the next schedule. That meant six months from then, and I expected to be transferred to the States before that time. I explained this to the examiner and, surprisingly, was allowed to finish that day's part of the examinations. That gave me a few days to try to get this sticky matter resolved.

On the way back to the base the thought came to me that since time was so short, I had to find another way to get permission to finish the exams. I was riding in the officers' launch crossing the bay to Sangley Point. One of my friends on board suggested I mention the problem to Admiral Olds as soon as we landed. That sounded logical. When I broached the subject to him, he said, "Well, let's see if we can get some help from our friend, General Aguinaldo."

Quite by accident, the Filipino statesman he was referring to was a former patient of mine. And I do mean "by accident," not luck. It was truly by God's appointment. A few months prior to this, the general, whose residence was in Kawit, Cavite near the Naval Base, had fallen in his home and fractured his wrist. Let me quote from another letter sent to my parents on June 29, 1949:

"I am now in the role of personal physician to the first president of the Republic of the Philippines,

General Emilio Aquinaldo. He, incidently, is the same man (now 81) who led the Filipinos in revolution against the U.S. when we first acquired these islands by conquering the Spaniards. He later became a staunch friend of his American 'over-lords' and has been a major influence in the Philippine political scene ever since. His name is mentioned in *Readers' Digest* under 'Uncle Sam's Imperialistic Jag.'

That retired general fell down a couple of steps and fractured his wrist Saturday morning. He was seen at a Manila hospital and told it was a sprain and a masseur was appointed. Our admiral visited him on Sunday and saw the bandaged wrist. Since he has a keen eye for public relations, he told the general that he would ask the Navy doctor to drop in and take a look, too.

About an hour later I saw him in his spacious home with its unique furnishings for which an antique dealer would give a tidy sum, and the reception was cordial. The general's wife is a very proper Filipina with the habits and dress befitting her position as one-time 'First Lady.'

I awaited their chauffeur to drive the old man to our place for an X-ray. It looked like more than a sprain to me and really was a fracture requiring a plaster cast. I drove out there for follow-up calls about twice a week and am taking Lenore next time to see their home. When I told the admiral of the fracture and treatment at a dinner party, he murmured with delight that the Navy had come to the rescue — such good politics!"

So this was no ordinary patient, Admiral Olds assured me. This takes us back in history to shortly after the Spanish-American War, at the beginning of the 20th century. As that war wound down in 1898, Admiral Dewey sailed with his fleet of U.S. ships into Manila

Bay. After destroying the Spanish Navy there, and after the U.S. Army cleared the islands of the Spanish troops, America found that it had on its hands in the Orient a protectorate nation, liberated from Spain: the Philippines.

"President McKinley had sincerely believed, as he said, 'There was nothing left for us to do but to take them all, and to educate the Filipinos, and uplift and civilize and Christianize them, and by God's grace to do the very best we could by them.'"[1]

That was *not* what the brave Filipino soldiers and officers expected. These stalwarts had stormed the battle fields alongside the American troops to liberate the Philippines from the oppressive rule of Spain and gain their freedom. With the defeat of the Spaniards who had been their over-lords for 400 years, Filipinos considered themselves free at last! Among their heroes were Generals Bonifacio and Emilio Aguinaldo y Famy.

Imagine their chagrin when they learned that America considered the Philippines a protectorate of the USA. In defiance, those heros led their countrymen in setting up their own Filipino government. They elected officers of the Republic of the Philippines and General Emilio Aguinaldo y Famy of Kawit, Cavite was their first president.

"After Rizal, Emilio Aguinaldo was the most outstanding figure in Philippine history. He was a full-blooded Tagalog from Cavite, in whose name the Filipino insurrection had been conducted. He had shown a certain talent for military tactics."[2]

That autonomous government had an army. They valiantly fought skirmishes with the Americans. Though futile, such defiance showed their distrust of outside rule and their longing for independence. Their revolt was suppressed, but not the spirit of their cause.

"After Funston [commander of the USA forces] had captured Aguinaldo by a daring ruse, he gave him parole, and from that moment Aquinaldo became a loyal citizen, who did his utmost to help build up the

[1] Victor Heiser, M.D., *An American Doctor's Odyssey*; W.W. Norton & Co., Inc. 1936, page 47

[2] Ibid., page 57

31

islands."³

So the *Independistas* officially submitted to American colonial rule under a benevolent governor. Eventually Aguinaldo warmed to the American officials who took office. Nevertheless, independence was a burning issue which strained Philippine-American relations for all of the years of U.S. control.

"William Howard Taft was sent to the Islands early in 1900 to head a Commission of Five, two of whom were to become governors after him — Luke E. Wright, Secretary of Commerce and Police, and Henry C. Ide, Secretary of Finance and Justice. Their conception of their responsibilities included immediate attention to the material and physical needs of the Filipinos. Money was appropriated for roads and for improving Manila harbor, a thousand American school teachers were imported, a whole new system of government with its manifold ramifications was designed and executed. At the outset, Taft enunciated that the American goal in the Philippines was to train the Filipinos to self government as quickly as possible."⁴

Taft invited American Protestant missionaries to join this reformation process as teachers of public schools and colleges and seminaries. That was a major adjustment because Roman Catholicism had been the state religion for 400 years under Spain. Parish priests dominated every facet of life.

Because of this form of tyranny, Dr. Jose Rizal raised his voice — and pen. He wrote two novels which depicted living conditions during those times: *Nole Me Tangere* and *El Filibusterismo.* Because of his activism, he paid the supreme sacrifice before a firing squad. An impressive monument stands over that site in Manila, and statues of Rizal still stand today as memorials in most town plazas throughout the Philippines.

Aguinaldo's countrymen fought alongside Americans again from 1941 to 1945 against the Japanese invaders. Many books have been

³ Ibid., page 48-49
⁴ Ibid., page 48-49

written about those war years and the major part these valiant Filipinos played. The cost in life was extremely high.

After the defeat of Japan and their signing of the official surrender documents on September 2, 1945, peace returned to the Philippines. Restoration of Manila began. Repairing the ravages of World War II throughout that tropical paradise took many more years. As their part in reparations, the Japanese government paid for clearing the sunken ships out of Manila Bay, which took ten years.

Thereafter, the Philippine nation enjoyed a peaceful transition to full independence, fulfilling the promise made by Taft, Governor of the Philippines in the early 1900s. A gala celebration marked the rebirth of the republic on its inauguration day, July 4, 1946. As American officials lowered the Stars and Stripes, Filipinos proudly saluted the raising of their flag in its place. That date has remained a holiday: *Philippine-American Friendship Day.* The date is *not* called Independence Day. *That* day is celebrated June 12: the date when Spanish rule ended and the Philippine republic had its first president, Emilio Aguinaldo.

General Aguinaldo remained a famous and respected statesman, loved by his countrymen and respected by his American neighbors at the U. S. Naval Air Station at Sangley Point, especially Admiral Olds. It was quite in order for the admiral to assume full responsibility for the medical care of his friend Emilio when he fell down the polished stairway of his home and fractured his arm around the age of 80.

The general made an uncomplicated recovery. The house calls we made were more like social occasions. Lenore and I enjoyed the hospitality of Mrs. Aguinaldo who insisted on serving *merienda* (an afternoon snack) before our departure. We sat around a large round dining room table made from a variety of Philippine mahogany hardwoods. The Aguinaldos had sent a similar table to the White House in Washington, D.C., as an official state gift.

That unusual friendship was a unique privilege, though it was quite "by accident." Little wonder, then, that Admiral Olds suggested I take my problem concerning the medical license matter to General Aguinaldo. Before we left his home that weekend of the medical exams, the general hand-wrote the following letter:

"25 Enero, 1950
Dr. Conrado E. Lorenzo,
Chairman, Board of Medical Examination
Manila

Mahal na Director:
Ang Americanong may...Dr. L.D. Nelson,
Teniente ng M.C., U.S.N. na nakagamot sa bali ng
aking kamay ay malugod ko pong ipinakikilala sa
inyo."

But it would be better if I just give you the translation of his letter. It was written in the national language of the Philippines, Tagalog. He addressed the letter to the chairman of the Board of Medical Examiners in Manila. Filipino colleagues put considerable effort into the translation, since it is written in an older and more formal Tagalog than is commonly spoken today. This was the result of their labor:

"25 January, 1950
Dr. Conrado E. Lorenzo,
Chairman, Board of Medical Examination
Manila

My dear Director:
The American who bears this letter, Dr. L. D. Nelson, Lieutenant of the Medical Corps, U.S.N., who treated my fractured arm, I sincerely introduce to you and entrust also, whose sincere intention is to treat here in the Philippines, and if necessary, he is willing to be interviewed or take the examination. A foremost gratitude from me who comes to you with fondness with this humble request,

(signed) E. Aguinaldo"

I took the letter to the office of the medical examiner. He didn't ask for any other papers. I was able to resume taking the examinations without missing a day. Now medical license number 10208, issued on 24 August, 1950 by the Board of Medical Examiners, authorizes me to unrestricted practice as a Physician and Surgeon in the Philippines. Among the signatures is the name Conrado E. Lorenzo — which was not *by accident*. Hanging alongside this official certificate on my office wall is that original letter from the general. Both are treasured souvenirs.

Lenore and I were in America when the medical examiner's office finally released the results of the examination. Our president declared U.S. military involvement in Korea in June 1950, which had prevented my release from military duty. The Navy issued orders for me to report to the Navy Department in Washington, D.C. in the late summer of 1950. From there the Department ordered me to the U.S. Naval Academy Hospital in Annapolis, Maryland where I gained valuable surgical training as I worked alongside more experienced surgeons.

We realized anew how true are the words we read in Romans 8:28:

> And we know that **all things** work together for good to them that love God, to them who are the called according to His purpose.

25, Enero, 1950.

Dr. Conrado E. Lorenzo,
Chairman Board of Medical Examination.
Manila.

Mahal na Director:

Ang Americanong may taglay nito, Dr. L. D. Nelson, Teniente ng M.C. U.S.N.R. na nakagamot sa bali ng aking kamay ay malugod ko pong ipinakikilala sa inyo at naipagtatagubilin tuloy na makapaking dingin lamang ang kanilang layunin para makapangamot dito sa atin sa Filipinas. At kung kailangan, si-lay handa namang palitis o examen.

Ang pananang pasasalamat ni tong magiliw na sumasainyo.

E. Aguinaldo

4

TRANSITION

"For I know the thoughts that I think toward you,
saith the LORD,
thoughts of peace, and not of evil, to give you an
expected end" (Jeremiah 29:11).

Annapolis, Maryland, home of the prestigious U. S. Naval Academy. What a prize! I could hardly believe my eyes when I received orders to report to the Naval Hospital on that campus. I was assigned to the surgical service. Experience here would count toward the accreditation which I desired to achieve in the specialty of surgery.

For the first several months we rented a private home in the city until medical officers' quarters became available on the Academy grounds. The accommodations were more than adequate for our family. By that time we had two children; our second child, David, was born shortly after our arrival in Annapolis. Linda was in her second year, eager to explore everything.

Living in this environment, we took interest in water sports. Part of a Navy officer's training included sailing in various types of vessels. I broadened my military education by learning how to skipper sailboats: the small sloop, and the larger yawl. We sailed on the beautiful Severne River which flows into the Chesapeake Bay a few miles downstream.

As a family, we also became quite efficient at crabbing. No, I don't mean Lenore and I upgraded our ability to argue. But in

Maryland, crabbing is almost a sport. We would throw a simple string bated with a chicken head or other tempting morsel over the seawall and let it rest on the river bottom. Then, by slowly winding in the string, the angler could catch a soft-shell crab or two clinging to the bait. Linda enjoyed this sort of outing even at the tender age of two.

None of us was eager to process the crabs for food, however. The idea of dropping the live crabs into a pot of boiling water seemed cruel. Furthermore, cracking open the shell and picking out the meat was quite a chore. But that's crabbing.

Our residence was several hundred yards across an expanse of grass and up a slight grade above the Severne River — a beautiful view from the front porch. One afternoon Lenore was outside hanging laundry while Linda scampered around the house and David rested in his play pen. It dawned on Lenore that she hadn't seen Linda for a longer time than it should take to make a circuit of the house. She called, then ran to search for her. Finally she saw her: a toddler in a yellow dress, running as fast as her little legs could take her down the slope toward the Severne River.

We think Lenore could have qualified in the Olympic 200 meter dash. I'm not sure which one was more frightened, Lenore or Linda. Each of them was out of breath: one from the running and the other from crying after a spanking. Mother and daughter returned to the house exhausted. We had learned another lesson the hard way.

Annapolis, capital of Maryland, is an historic and picturesque little city. The grounds of the U. S. Naval Academy are always immaculate. The academy is a great tourist attraction, especially when the midshipmen are on parade. We never tired of watching them. Another bonus in this appointment was that my parents lived in Salisbury, Maryland, only two hours' drive from the Academy. From a human viewpoint, we enjoyed a plush assignment.

Perhaps subtle influences were tempting us to reconsider our future: a Navy career versus missionary life. But we had "set our sails" and when the required years of duty were completed in the fall of 1951, the Navy accepted my resignation. I signed the papers and received an honorable discharge. We were civilians once again, ready for an assignment for missionary service.

For the next five months, we made our headquarters at my parents' home in Salisbury on the Delmarva Peninsula. We wrote churches with which we had been associated in former years, explaining our intention to serve God as medical missionaries under ABWE in the Philippines. Several churches or groups invited us to tell them about the proposed work.

About this time, ABWE informed us that a one-month orientation program for new missionaries was scheduled for that fall. We were requested to join that first class and we gladly accepted the invitation. Lenore's parents were willing to take the children for the month, since children could not be accommodated in the limited mission facilities. All missionary candidates from then on would have to spend time in orientation prior to appointment.

The orientation was designed to give candidates a more thorough introduction to ABWE and its principles and practices. Living as a group in those quarters, performing household and campus chores as part of the arrangement, would also indicate how cooperative the candidates might be in adapting to various situations. That was hardly the civilian equivalent of a "boot camp." The accommodations bordered on the luxurious to most of the candidates. No one suffered; everyone gained from the experience.

For us, it was a unique opportunity. We were already accepted by the mission, so we were "in." But the orientation proved invaluable. Our hostess was a veteran missionary, Ruth Woodworth, who had served in the Philippines in the pre-war years. As a group we memorized the fourth chapter of Second Corinthians. This remains an indelible treasure in my brain and heart.

When we first signed on with ABWE we had been appointed to serve in Dutch New Guinea. Now came the transition from a New Guinea mindset to the appointment to the Philippines. But the necessity for this was obvious: the Dutch Religious Consul in Batavia, who controlled all religious works in the Dutch East Indies, would not accept the application of a new mission agency.

One of the original appointees to the team, Gerald Rose, did go to New Guinea under the auspices of an approved mission, the Christian and Missionary Alliance. He later united with that agency and married one of its members. Perhaps some people are more innovative than others. I prefer to credit God with Rose's decision.

I have observed that missionaries often have difficulty shifting gears if field assignments are changed. That wasn't traumatic for Lenore and me, having been in the Philippines. We felt that God had given us the Navy duty there for that specific reason. But others find such an adjustment difficult. They may even question God's leading. Surely the Lord of the harvest knows best where an individual will be the most productive and bring the most glory to God. Jesus said in John 15:8, 16:

> Herein is my Father glorified, that ye bear much fruit; so shall ye be my disciples... Ye have not chosen me, but I have chosen you and ordained you that ye should go and bring forth fruit, and that your fruit should remain.

If you want to observe an effective missionary who had many changes of venue, study the life of the apostle Paul. He accepted the fact that sometimes the Spirit of the Lord granted him opportunity for service, and at other times He did not. Nevertheless, Paul tried the doors till they opened or closed. He went in the direction God chose. God said about Paul,

> ".. .he is a chosen vessel unto me, to bear my name before the Gentiles, and kings, and the children of Israel" (Acts 9:15).

God's assignment for Paul was *general* and not specific from the very beginning. God continues to seek witnesses who have willing heart to serve Him "in Jerusalem, and in all Judea, and in Samaria, and unto the uttermost part of the earth" (Acts 1:8).

God knows best the place and time He can use us. As an illustration, a surgeon uses a variety of instruments to accomplish his purpose. The doctor chooses the one that suits his need at that moment. He only requires that the instruments be clean, sharp, and readily available.

> I beseech you therefore, brethren, by the mercies of God, that ye present your bodies a living sacrifice, holy, acceptable unto God, which is your reasonable service. And be not conformed to this world: but be ye transformed by the renewing of your mind, that ye may prove what is that good, and acceptable, and perfect, will of God (Romans 12:1-2).
>
> I keep under my body, and bring it into subjection: lest by any means when I have preached to others, I myself should be a castaway [disqualified] (1 Corinthians 9:27).

That last verse does not imply that the person whom God judges "disqualified" has lost his salvation, but that he has marred his testimony to the extent he cannot be used. The surgeon sets aside an instrument for repair. Sometimes that may mean it can no longer be used for its intended purpose. Unfortunately, examples of "disqualified" Christian leaders can be seen with increasing frequency. Even missionaries, pastors, or teachers may be set on the shelf, so to speak, because of immorality or other sinful behavior.

On the other hand, however, let me recall an example of a missionary who was *not* disqualified from future leadership, though he had failed a test. His name was John Mark.

In Matthew 27 we learn that Mark's mother was Mary. She undoubtedly was among the many women who followed Jesus and helped supply His material needs. Later, her home was the place where Christ's followers met for prayer (Acts 12:12). So Mark was taught the scriptures early in life. As a young man, he apparently followed Jesus and the disciples quite regularly. He was probably with them in Gethsemane when Jesus was apprehended by the mob. His uncle was Joseph of Cyprus, a Levite who was called Barnabas (the Encourager) in Acts 11:22-24.

After the resurrection and ascension of Jesus, Mark joined his uncle and Paul on a missionary journey. He saw the hardships that those missionaries encountered. Apparently the exposure was too much for him as a youth, and he dropped out rather abruptly somewhere along the line (Acts 13:13). Perhaps he was frightened and/or homesick. Whatever it was, he quit. He'd *had* it! True, he failed the test, but scripture does not suggest that he had disqualified himself.

The next time Doctor Luke, the author of the book of Acts, mentioned John Mark's name, Paul and Barnabas were preparing for a second missionary trip. Barnabas suggested that they take Mark with them again. Paul refused. Their disagreement was so severe that they broke up the team and formed two others: one headed by Paul, who took on Silas; Barnabas took Mark, willing to give the young man a chance to prove himself.

We don't hear much about that experience, but we find that Mark did persevere. He must have stood the test. His spiritual stamina was strengthened. I believe some time later he was discipled by the apostle Peter, who understood what it was like to be considered a failure, for Peter referred to Mark as "my son" (1 Peter 5:13). That mature man with sensitivity coached the errant youth into realizing a beautiful, productive life.

Whatever happened, Mark proved faithful for the apostle Paul in prison later wrote: "Take Mark, and bring him with thee: for he is profitable to me for the ministry" (2 Timothy 4:11). Imagine that. Paul, of all people wanted Mark! He even wrote a recommendation for him to the church at Colosse in which he said that Mark was "... a fellow-worker unto the kingdom of God, who has been a comfort unto me" (Colossians 4:10,11). So Paul must have requested Mark to stay with him as a companion even in a prison cell.

The capstone of John Mark's usefulness came when he was entrusted to be the author of the second of the four gospels, under the inspiration of the Holy Spirit. He recorded the life of his Master, Jesus Christ. Young Mark's experience teaches us about an ongoing need for mature Christians to encourage young men and women who have stumbled or failed in their walk with the Lord.

What if Barnabas had *not* given John Mark a second chance?
What if Paul had insisted on preaching to the Jews only?
What if we had insisted on going to Dutch New Guinea?

5
LOST AND FOUND

"To everything there is a season,
and a time to every purpose under heaven:
... a time to get and a time to lose;
a time to keep and a time to cast away" (Ecclesiastes 3:1,6).

Have you ever experienced that sickening feeling that hits you right in the pit of the stomach? You enter a classroom for the final exams and you can't even remember your name, much less the answers you must give to those questions coming up. Perhaps that how you feel when standing on the tower preparing to bungee-jump. Or, after cleaning out the garage or attic, separating boxes and trash for burning, you discover that you have accidentally burned up an irreplaceable treasured gift from a loved one.

That's how I felt in the middle of the night on an inter-island ship out in the middle of Manila Bay. It was April 1952.

Lenore and I had completed the circuit of churches and had gained the required basic financial support. We had said our tearful good-byes to our parents and friends. My father's words still warmed our hearts. When his friends asked if our leaving to be missionaries wasn't too hard to bear, he would reply, "No, I would rather have them ten thousand miles from home, *in the center of God's will*, than living across the street." Now we were in the Philippines as missionaries.

We had arrived in Manila after sailing for 16 days across the Pacific on the *M/V LAURA MAERSK*, a Norwegian freighter. Those ships carry only twelve passengers along with their primary purpose: hauling cargo. That creates a more informal and intimate group of travelers than the larger and more luxurious passenger ships. Besides, all our worldly goods were on board, including a Jeep station wagon outfitted as a medical emergency vehicle.

For the few days in Manila, we were guests of our old friends and fellow missionaries, Bernard and Eleanor Bancroft. They had met our ship, and helped us through the paper work of entry into the country. Our cargo was transferred to the inter-island ship. Now we were on our way to the southern island of Mindanao, by way of the city of Cebu where the freight would have to clear customs.

The night we were to sail, a taxi had picked us up at the Bancrofts' house and had taken us to the pier. Lenore and I grabbed our hand bags and the two children, Linda (two years old) and David (just past his first birthday). It was late, so we hurried on board and were taken to our cabin. The cabin was adequate for our family with two double-decker bunks. The kids were soon in their night gear and put to bed. We followed shortly thereafter.

As I lay pondering the day's excitement, the thought of our clearing customs in Cebu City crossed my mind. The passports and papers that were necessary for clearance were safely in the briefcase. *The BRIEFCASE!*

"Lenore, where did you put the briefcase?" I asked.

"I didn't touch your briefcase. Don't you have it?" was her sleepy reply. My drowsiness was immediately dispelled.

I dropped to the deck and began the search. No briefcase in the cabin. "Now I remember. I had it in the taxi and put it behind my legs in the front seat while I held Linda on my lap. I must have left it in the cab!" The reputation of cab drivers is known around the world. What was the likelihood that we'd ever see those valuables again? And how does one go about replacing shipping papers, packing lists, passport documents and the like?

By this time, the ship was nearing Corregidor Island at the mouth of Manila Bay, made famous as the last headquarters of General Douglas MacArthur prior to his evacuation to Australia when the

Japanese over-ran the Philippines in early 1942. General Wainwright and his men surrendered to the enemy forces shortly thereafter. I was about to surrender to the inevitable, too, *"... a time to search, and a time to give up as lost."* Perhaps I could empathize with the general just a bit better, under these circumstances.

In a desperate mood, I dressed and went up to the bridge. When I told the captain my story, he had one of the sailors take me to the purser's office. He seemed sympathetic enough and took me to the radio operator on board. I wrote out a message to Bernie Bancroft, stating our plight. The radio man got busy on the telegraph key and sent the news by Morris Code. Now all that was left for us to do was to *pray*. And that we did, as often as our restless night brought us back to consciousness.

I had plenty of time during that cruise to write a letter to the folks back home:

> "Only one thing mars the trip, and that is due to my stupidity, or something. We had about 19 pieces of luggage to bring aboard, so we loaded Bernard's car to get them to the pier at sailing time. That filled the car, so Eleanor, Lenore, the kids and I took a taxi and went ahead of Bernard. I had not trusted my briefcase to anyone all along those past 10,000 miles because it contained all the vital papers. So it was with me in the taxi, but in the confusion of paying the driver and unloading, I completely forgot the briefcase. It remained in the cab as we pulled out of the harbor, and no doubt even the driver didn't find it for some time, unless he stopped suddenly and it thumped to the floor.

> The contents include our passports, immigration papers, medical registration, tax receipts, listings of the contents of all our crates, and our address book. It has another vital paper: a customs department exemption on household effects and medical supplies contained in the Cebu crates. We must clear them

with customs tomorrow before we can take them with us to Cagayan de Oro and then up to Malaybalay. Whether customs will clear us at all without a copy of the bill-of-lading is a major concern. I think we'll have to go to Malaybalay without the crates until I can get the papers straightened out again. That may take time, now that we will be 400 miles (640 kilometers) from Manila and about 7,000 islands apart.

We've been much in prayer and are giving you these details in order that you and the home churches can pray about it. No cash was in the bag, but much time, labor, frustration and expense went into getting those documents. The recovery of the briefcase depends on the integrity of the cab driver. I radioed Bancrofts within an hour after sailing and gave them the details on which to work. Now we are waiting for the Lord's help."

The ship sailed for 36 hours among the beautiful emerald islands to the port of Cebu City. The ship tied up to the pier and we prepared to disembark. When the cabin attendant came to assist in the process, he brought a telegram addressed to us. It read:

"PICK UP BRIEF CASE AT CEBU AIRPORT (SIGNED) **BANCROFT"**

So much for the rumor that taxi drivers are not honest. The taxi driver who drove us to the pier in Manila found the briefcase where I had left it, remembered where he had picked us up, and took it to Bancroft's house. Bernie saw to it that it was on board the Philippine Airlines plane for Cebu the next morning — hand-carried by the pilot!

Nothing was missing! The passports and documents were intact. You probably could have heard our shouts of praise and thanksgiving clear back in the USA, had you been listening. Clearing customs was a breeze following that excitement. After another overnight on the ship, we arrived at our destination on the north coast of Mindanao: Cagayan de Oro City. From there, we trucked our cargo 70 miles

(112 kilometers) south to the city of Malaybalay where we lived for the next 25 years.

LOST and FOUND — when Jesus was in His itinerant ministry for three years, He related several parables. Among them are the parables of the lost *sheep*, the lost *silver* and the lost *son* (also known as *the prodigal*). They are recorded for us in Luke chapter 15. The lessons derived from those *"lost things"* include:

* In each instance, the thing lost was just one of many. This speaks to me of the evident *uniqueness* of the object of concern. Though there were many sheep, many coins and more than one son, yet the lost ones were very important to the ones doing the searching. Each of the lost items had special, intrinsic worth.

* In each instance, the *superb intensity* of the search was constant. No hardship along the trail was too difficult for the shepherd as he searched for the lost sheep. The pain produced by the thorny bushes didn't deter the concerned seeker. The housewife spent all her energy upturning the furniture, regardless of the aching muscles. The father waited at home with his eyes on the horizon every day and lights on every night so that his son would know he was welcome to return.

* In each instance, the *joy of recovery* was immense: the lost was found! It couldn't be contained in isolation. It was party time with family and friends in celebration of the event!

Jesus meant those parables to point up the fact that "there is joy in the presence of the angels of God over one sinner who repents" (Luke 15:10). Each of us is unique; each of us is *"hounded"* by God until found; and heaven rejoices at the results. The *purpose of missions* is to unite believers in Christ in the search for lost souls.

As fishermen use different methods and differing bait to catch fish, so there are different strategies in missionary work. Some have criticized medical missions as being too much social gospel. Indeed, it can be. In the early part of the 20th century when missionaries were invited by then-President William McKinley to carry the gospel to the Philippines, 25 church-related hospitals were built. At first they may have had an evangelistic thrust, but when you visit those hospitals still operating today, you will be hard pressed to find any evidence of active evangelistic effort. Their primary concern seems to be in meeting physical need. They exemplify the "social gospel" approach.

The ABWE hospitals, on the other hand, have maintained the priority of searching for the lost to bring them to Jesus Christ as Lord and Savior in humble confession of sin and repentance that leads to salvation. At the time of this writing, the Philippine hospitals which were established for the most part by ABWE are owned and operated by Bible-believing Filipino Christians under independent boards of trustees. These individuals maintain the same goals of professional excellence and a spiritual emphasis as those of the missionary founders.

To support that claim, let me share excerpts from the December '93 *HEART BEAT* newsletter of Bethel Baptist Hospital:

"We saw 665 patient-professions of faith in the Lord during 1993. In June the Philippine General Hospital's internship program began sending interns here to gain experience. Six medical students have come to Bethel for this six-week course. They treated and lived with native Bukidnons in rural villages for ten days for their community outreach. Their remaining time was spent at the Bethel Baptist Hospital. Most, if not all of them, have recognized the need of having a personal relationship with the Lord Jesus Christ.

Those young energetic doctors were such an encouragement to the staff. They blended with the work force and had a stamina and dedication to the work. They were really extraordinary. More than half of them had personally accepted Christ" (as recorded in a note by Alfred Aguilar).

"Hi! I'm Susan, born and bred in Manila, one of the new faces in the BBH family. Okay, now you're wondering why a city girl is among the mountains of Bukidnon. Well, it all started with a commitment I made to the Lord to serve in a mission hospital while I was still in medical school. So, here I am eight months later, having no regrets.

I praise and thank our Lord Jesus Christ for bringing me here because He has taught me the essence of being a Christian doctor. From day one of work here, I have learned the meaning of Galatians 5:22,23: love, joy, peace, patience, kindness, goodness, faithfulness, gentleness, and self-control. Those are the traits that a Christian doctor must reveal. But to have all those is impossible on our own: we must have a personal relationship with Jesus Christ as our own Savior and Lord, and be submissive to His will. Ministering to the needs of the patients is not enough: they must be treated with love and compassion — just as Jesus did when He healed during His time here on earth.

The Lord has truly blessed me through my work here and through the people of BBH and Malaybalay. Every day has been very enriching and exciting! There is one important truth that I have discovered and will always remember: I am just a hemline of Jesus' garment, a mere instrument of His healing power. God is the GREAT PHYSICIAN!" (by Susan P., M.D.)

"As an employee of Bethel Baptist Hospital, I am most thankful to our Heavenly Father for sending the American missionaries here to spread the Gospel and start a medical missions work in Malaybalay. The older female employees in this hospital are fortunate to be part of this ministry because we have a great privilege to work in spite of our insufficient academic background. Most of us started our services at the hospital during the 1960s; and some of us are still here because of God's grace. We work happily serving the Lord no matter what the difficulties ..." (by Norma S.)

We felt that it was party-time when that lost briefcase of ours was returned. What must heaven be like? Is it an on-going party time with Jesus Christ and His angelic host because of those precious ones who were **LOST BUT NOW ARE FOUND?**

6

"YOU WILL JUST BE THE ONE"

"... He hath sent me to heal the *broken-hearted*,
... and recovering of sight to the *blind*,
to set at liberty them that are *bruised*" (Luke 4:18).

THE BLIND

Blindness is rampant in the tropics. The causes are manifold. Some children are born with eye defects and never see the light of day, or they see only varying shades of gray. Others are born of infected mothers and develop severe eye infections with ugly results. Corneal ulcers may be one of the damaging aspects of childhood diseases such as measles or chicken-pox; more often blindness is a result of injury — from a sharp blade of grass or a stick striking the cornea. The central vision is lost.

Adults often are afflicted with glaucoma and may lose their vision rapidly, accompanied by severe headaches and eye pain. But this condition sometimes starts painlessly. Gradual loss of vision is often the earliest sign — at first peripheral vision is lost, then slowly creeping more centrally until there is total blindness. Another condition causing blindness is a small tumor at the junction of the two optic nerves producing characteristic "tunnel vision" which allows the patient to see only straight ahead. Occasionally optic neuritis in one or both eyes destroys vision, and that permanently. Nutritional deficiencies may be at the root of this and other types of blindness. The best known example of this is vitamin A deficiency which produces "night blindness," which is especially prevalent in children in Third-World countries.

Then there is a slowly developing blindness from damage to the retina — the lining of the eyeball — from a variety of causes, including diabetes and high blood pressure. I'll not forget examining one man's eyes. He came to the clinic in Leyte complaining that he was slowly and painlessly losing his vision. When I peered through his dilated pupils with an ophthalmoscope, I found the retina of each eye streaked with an incurable type of inflammation: *retinitis pigmentosa*. He could barely see and his future of total blindness was only a matter of time. As calmly as I could, I asked, "Where do you live, and what do you do for a living?"

His reply floored me, "Oh, I'm just visiting here and my friend suggested I ask you to see what's wrong before I return to Manila. I am a taxi driver in the city!" I wondered how many others in his profession were similarly afflicted. That would help to explain their driving habits: the way they so calmly cut in and out of traffic, and make their own rules as they go. They are all blind. Of course, I'm exaggerating. We can't blame bad driving on poor eyesight alone.

I also learned more about another severe eye condition while filling in for one of the mission doctors in Togo, West Africa. The common term for the malady is river blindness. The scientific name for the condition is *onchocerciasis*, so called that because it is caused by a parasite that gets into the tissues of the patient and migrates to various parts of the body, often including the eyes.

The name river blindness is derived from the life cycle of this parasite. A tiny black fly, a species called *Simulium damnosum* (obviously named by some distraught scientist), breeds along the banks of fast flowing rivers in Africa and some parts of South America. It is only one to five millimeters in length, so its size is considerably smaller than the average house fly. The black fly does not enter houses but bites people out-of-doors during the daylight hours. Furthermore, not only is it a pest afflicting people that live along the river, but also those living as far as 250 miles (400 kilometers) from its breeding place.

When these flies bite an unsuspecting person who already is

afflicted with the disease of *onchocerciasis* and is working in the fields or resting under some tree, a form of the parasite is sucked into the fly's body. Within about ten days it develops into a larval form which can be passed along to the fly's next victim. In the new host these microscopic larvae set up nests in the skin. Eventually the patient experiences intense itching. It is during the parasite's migration that damage occurs to the eyes. Later the patient notices small lumps just under the surface of the skin as the parasites mature into adult forms. To make the diagnosis, the laboratory technician nicks the skin with a sharp blade and examines under the microscope the droplet of fluid that is obtained. The wriggling microfilaria, when present, are readily visible.

In 1986 the World Health Organization (WHO) estimated that 18 million people are infected with this parasite. One way to prevent this disease is to control the vector, the black fly. Prompted by President Carter, WHO started the Onchocerciasis Control Programme (OCP) in 1975, using low flying aircraft to spray insecticides along the river banks. But an even more important breakthrough was the discovery that a drug, ivermectin, used in veterinary medicine for parasitic diseases in animals, is effective in humans afflicted with river blindness. Hospitals in West Africa now use this as the first line of treatment.

The patient highlighted in this chapter is a rather frail little woman in the Philippines. She was led over the trails from her mountain *barrio* about a day's journey to Bethel clinic in Malaybalay. She could only discern light. She was afflicted with one of the most frequent causes of blindness in adults: cataracts. The lens of each eye was opaque, making the pupils look grayish-white instead of a glossy black. Sometimes that type of lens is called a sugar cube because of its typical appearance. Probably the hot tropical sun's ultraviolet rays have something to do with this condition.

I explained to this sweet little grandmother that she needed an operation on at least one of her eyes. Only then would she see again. After surgery, she would have to wear thick glasses to see clearly. Furthermore, I informed her that the nearest eye surgeon was in the city of Cagayan de Oro on the coast, about a 70 miles (112 kilometers) north.

She smiled sweetly and replied in her native Binokid dialect, "You will just do it here." To her this made good sense. She had never been that far away from her home in all of her 60 years. So why should she break that record now? I went over the same explanation again, concluding with, "I'm not a specialist in eye surgery. This is a delicate kind of operation, and you need an expert to do it."

"You will just be the one," was her monotonous response after each attempt to make her understand the matter. She would not budge from her decision. I was reminded of Jesus' parable in the book of Luke, chapter 18: *the widow who would not take "No" for the answer.* Day after day she returned to a judge who was not inclined to listen to her grievance. But he finally gave in to her request, just to get her off his back. In frustration, I asked my patient to give me time to think it over and then return for my answer. She and her family moved to a house nearby.

Incidentally, this was a common practice. A family member, or possibly all of the immediate family of a patient would accompany him/her to the hospital. If prolonged treatment was required for several weeks, they would move nearby. Some stayed with friends or relatives, while others had to find appropriate lodging elsewhere. For this reason, our mission hospital constructed a motel-like structure: eight rooms without furniture, plus a community cooking area. The caretaker was one of the church members. I would have referred to him as the overseer of the building if it weren't for the fact that he was totally blind himself. He kept things in order, nevertheless, thanks to his remaining senses and indomitable spirit.

Of course, in my surgical training years I had rotated through all of the departments and assisted in surgery on patients with cataracts and other operable eye conditions. I knew, or thought I knew, that I wouldn't be doing those operations but only referring such patients to the specialists. Now here we were, just beginning our missionary career in a remote town in the middle of Mindanao, with no ophthalmologist.

For the next several days I poured over the text book on eye surgery, which was happily included in our shipment of supplies. I found that we did have the basic set of instruments, so I couldn't use that excuse for not doing the surgery. What I needed was the *feel* of the procedure. So I sent an attendant to the market in town and told him to buy a few eyes of slaughtered animals. Now I had plenty of material upon which to practice — painlessly.

My Binokid patient returned. She anticipated a favorable response from me. I told her that I would do the surgery; however, I emphasized the possibility of her losing what vision she had. She didn't take long to decide: she insisted, "You will just be the one!" I remembered an old proverb I had heard while still in the Navy: "Fools rush in where angels fear to tread." My mind reasoned on that occasion, " I'm *not* rushing in. I'm dragging my heels!"

The day came for the surgery. Lenore and Davie, another ABWE nurse, had things ready. We placed the patient on the table and positioned the battery-powered operating light. As was our custom before starting any surgical procedure, I prayed audibly for the patient and for those of us helping her that God's hand would rest upon ours and His will be done.

With text book opened nearby, I began. To my delight, all went according to instructions. The bandage was applied and the patient was ever-so-gently placed in the recovery room bed. Both the patient and her attendant were told that she must keep her head perfectly still for the next 48 hours, and sandbags were adjusted to help her keep that position. Now we had a five day wait before we would know the outcome.

That big day finally came. As I unwrapped the circular bandage dressing, none of us breathed. Would she see or not? The last bit of covering was removed. Silence. Then the smiling little mountaineer cried, "You're white!" She made our day. A few more days of recovery were allowed before she left for home. She was told to come back for a check-up in a couple of months. Off she went, and no one had to lead her by the hand.

Upon her return we found that healing was progressing nicely and to complete the recovery, Ron found a pair of glasses which had been worn by another cataract patient postoperatively. They fit her just right. How precious is the gift of physical sight!

I don't know who was the happiest: the patient or we who were the instruments God used to help "open blind eyes." I've always been grateful to that simple mountain woman who insisted that I "just be the one" to do the surgery.

Since then many patients with eye problems have been operated on in our mission hospitals. A devout Chinese Christian, Dr. Tony Lim, a specialist in eye-ear-nose-throat (EENT) surgery, flew to Malaybalay from the city of Davao for a few days of consultations every other month. By assisting him in such cases, I was able to improve my technique. Years later, Dr. Bob Smith, a Canadian ophthalmologist, flew to the Philippines on several occasions to perform eye surgery. During his visit, he concentrated on training me further until I was ready to take over the surgical care of patients with eye problems. Few operations bring more satisfaction to both patient and surgeon than opening blind eyes.

In reviewing Luke 18 again, I was impressed with the account in verses 35-43 of another person whose blind eyes had been opened. He, too, had been insistent that he be seen by the itinerant Healer passing his way. He kept calling out, "Jesus, Son of David, have mercy on me!"

Jesus stopped and asked a question that might at first seem strange: "What do you want me to do for you?" Certainly, the incarnate Son of God knew what this beggar wanted. But the more I meditate on this story, the more I realize that this beggar, named Bartimaeus, had to sort out the difference between wants and needs. Being a beggar who daily sat at the roadside awaiting hand-outs from those who passed by, one might assume that he wanted Jesus to add more coins to rattle in his cup — material gain.

But no, that was not what he *needed*: "Lord, I want to receive my sight!" And he knew in his heart who could heal him.

Jesus acted on the beggar's *faith*: "Receive your sight; your faith has made you well." Then we read, "Immediately he received his

Link attended medical college as a midshipman in the U.S. Navy from 1943 to 1946.

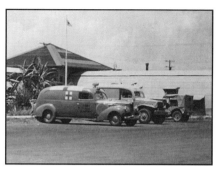

The Naval Hospital, Sangley Point, Cavite, Philippines where Linda was born in August 1949, and where Link was the medical officer from 1949 to 1951.

Our first term with ABWE ended with our family including Linda, David and baby Sandra.

Young David Nelson and his little friend Moomoy.

General Emilio Aguinaldo had his fractured arm treated by Link while at the U.S. Naval Air Base in 1949.

Myra Lou Barnard (R) and partner Jan Forster return to their translation work after the fire.

Above left: The Aunties" Millie Crouch and Priscilla Bailey. Above: The Aunties try their hand at cooking on a native fire table during a Short-term Institute.

Dr. Bill Stevenson took unto himself a wife and had an instant family of 10.

Dr. Tony Maravilla, his wife Diane, and their miracle daughter Dawn.

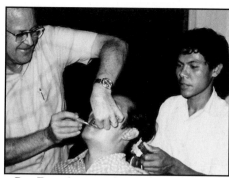

Ron Esson became adept at dental extractions.

The Manobo warrior who recovered from the goring by a wild boar. "Pigs is pigs!"

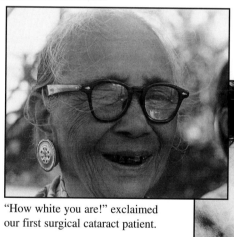

"How white you are!" exclaimed our first surgical cataract patient.

Eunice praised God for her leprosy because it led her to Bethel Baptist Clinic where she accepted Christ as her Savior.

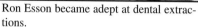

The missionaries prepare to hike to another mountain village for a Bible Institute. Pictured from left: Filipino guides, Rosemary Ullery, Doris Shoemaker, Lenore and Link with a couple of the kids.

Ella Grover begins laboratory tests on Ruth Woodworth in Bethel Baptist Hospital's lab.

Lenore and Gene Ebersole were close friends. Mother's Day of 1965 in Baguio.

Cool water soothes sore feet during the hike.

sight, and began following Him, glorifying God; and when all the people saw it, they gave praise to God."

Bartimaeus didn't need glasses to see clearly. When Jesus opened his eyes they could see 20/20. Imagine how he must have danced around Jericho! Wherever he went, he bore witness to the fact that his friend and healer, Jesus, was God incarnate.

Jesus is still in the business of opening blind eyes — spiritually blind eyes, that is. The problem is that so many wander through life thinking that all they need are more temporal things rather than that which is eternal. Jesus said, "Seek ye *first* the kingdom of God, and His righteousness; and all these *things* shall be added to you" (Matthew 6:33). Where are *your* priorities?

THE BURDENED

Another patient came to us who wouldn't take "No" for an answer. His name was Trecente, a 12-year-old boy. He had a tumor on his right leg the size of a watermelon. It weighed over sixteen pounds, stretched from his knee to his ankle, and measured twelve inches across. What a burden that was for a boy to carry around! Besides, his mother had to alter his pant-leg on the right. He could only wear shorts that had the seam opened so that he could button them along the side.

We asked his father, "Why did you wait so long before having this operated on?" We knew he could have taken the boy to the coast to see a surgeon in one of the bigger hospitals. Perhaps the expense was too much to bear. But I wasn't quite prepared for his answer:

"I took him to the doctors, but all they could do for him would be to cut off his leg. I wouldn't agree to that. So if you will save his leg, you will just be the one." Where had I heard that before?

I checked the boy over. He was thin from carrying his tumor around and from not eating a nutritious diet. But on the whole, his heart and blood tests confirmed that he could withstand surgery. After a day or two of preparation, he was taken to our operating room. I injected the spinal anesthetic. The mass was obviously a benign tumor composed of fatty tissue — a lipoma. The bulk of it was on the front of the leg so that the major vessels and nerves were not affected. We worked painstakingly for about six hours. Since a spinal anesthetic only lasts about two to three hours at the most, I had to give repeated doses. With analgesics to supplement the anesthetic, he was comfortable and withstood the operation well.

As the operation progressed, it was interesting to see that the pressure on the tibia over the years had caused it to bow appreciably and to thin out like a saber. Nevertheless, the leg was saved and the vital blood and nerve supply were undamaged. We applied a bandage and placed him in his bed.

The parents were grateful to the point of tears when they saw the mass gone and the leg intact. But the boy experienced a greater relief: he thought his leg would just float off the bed, it was so light. The burden was gone. He hadn't realized how heavy it was, since it had grown so slowly during the ten years. But now — what a difference! He could walk and run and even wear regular pants again, just like the other boys.

Trecente and his parents stayed with us until he had fully healed. During that time the family heard repeatedly the good news: the burden of sin which weighs upon the heart can also be removed. They listened and heeded. They asked God to forgive their sin, and He did. That's what medical missions is all about!

THE BROKEN

A carefully planned day is good time management. But emergencies do occur, especially in medical work. Nevertheless, we tried our best to get rest-breaks scheduled into each day, each week and each year.

We needed an afternoon break of an hour or two every day while living in the tropics. The hours between noon and two o'clock were usually *siesta* hours. Even the shop-keepers took naps. We learned not to go to the market if we wanted to be waited on during those hours.

Besides that, we took a full day off every week. I advocate this practice for every new missionary. At first, energetic young people come to their mission stations with the idea that such a practice is only for the aged and infirm. Those who disregarded my advice sometimes fell victims of heat exhaustion or early burn-out.

To complete the picture, families living in the tropics need an *annual* vacation away from home for a month, preferably in a cooler environment. That schedule undoubtedly kept us going longer and in better health than some of our colleagues who ignored the advice. ABWE advocates the implementation of such a policy.

But schedules are bound to be broken by emergencies. We found this out early in our career on more than one occasion. The best way for us to really get a break was to get up early and drive off to a distant place for a picnic and family fun.

One emergency caught us while still at home. A weary man came to our door and called, *"Maayo!"* (pronounced ma-*eye*-o). In some countries, a visitor will simply call or clap his hands to be noticed, rather than knock on the door. Apparently that was the custom in Christ's day, too, for in one of His parables He mentions the neighbor who *called* in the middle of the night until his sleeping friend awoke to give him what he needed. We could empathize with that weary friend.

When we heard a man calling at our door, "Sir, you will be the one to take care of our boy," we knew that ended our day off. He quickly told us the reason for his urgent visit.

This man's 12-year-old nephew was stripping abaca fiber when he was dragged into the machinery of the mill. Abaca is the tough fiber used to make hemp rope. It must be stripped from the stalk, similar to that of banana plants. The boy's arm had been caught in the belt of the machine. They finally had been able to free him, but he fainted when they tried to move him. They couldn't carry the boy because of his broken bones and they couldn't dial 9-1-1.

After a quick lunch, we packed up the emergency equipment, and I drove the uncle in our Jeep station wagon. Several hours later, thanks to four-wheel drive, we arrived in a remote village only to learn that it was another hour's hike to the plantation where the lad lay. Several helpers carried the equipment, including a stretcher and a pressure lantern. We anticipated that nightfall might find us still on the trail.

Barking dogs announced our approach to the bamboo-and-thatch house. We climbed the ladder and found wall-to-wall adults and children on the floor, arousing from sleep. The patient was bundled up in one corner. My hasty examination confirmed a fractured arm as well as concussion and multiple bruises. I dressed the wounds and stabilized the arm in a splint, preparatory to moving him onto the stretcher for the trip back to the clinic.

But a congregation that size was not to be neglected, so we held a short gospel service before leaving. I told of the One who knew what it was to suffer, for He was "broken" for the sin of the world: Jesus Christ. Isaiah prophesied this and wrote:

> He was wounded for our transgressions, he was *bruised* for our iniquities: the chastisement of our peace was upon him; and with his stripes (scourging) we are healed (Isaiah 53:5).

The apostle Paul wrote concerning Jesus on the day prior to his death. He instituted the ordinance known as the Lord's Supper, which we still celebrate:

> The Lord Jesus the same night in which he was betrayed took bread: and when he had given thanks, he broke it, and said, "Take, eat: this is my body, which is *broken* for you: this do in remembrance of me" (1 Corinthians 11:23-24).

We began our trek back through the jungle with men carrying the patient on a stretcher. After midnight we arrived at the house where we left the Jeep. We slept until daybreak before driving home, arriving just in time to carry on the regular morning clinic already in progress. We reduced the boy's fracture and placed his arm in a cast. Within a month his arm healed and we removed the plaster cast. Furthermore, the seed of God's Word had penetrated his soul. We were confident that it would sprout. Considering all those friends and relatives whose hearts were also "good soil", I believe our day off was God's day on.

House calls are a thing of the past, even for most missionary doctors. But during the first few years, I made many visits to patients

WITH SCALPEL AND THE SWORD

in their homes. As I reflect upon the relationships built while treating the patient in his home, I can see the wisdom of making house calls. The patient's living conditions and interpersonal relationships contribute to or endanger the patient's well-being. Accepting hospitality in the patient's home creates a bond between the doctor and the patient's entire *family*. Much of that is lost today in the hustle and bustle of life in Western society, sacrificing compassion on the altar of efficiency. In the Philippines we often heard the expression, "You will just be the one." Now I know what it means.

7
APPROPRIATE IN ITS TIME

"To everything there is a season,
and a time to every purpose under the heavens:
... a time to weep, and a time to laugh;
a time to mourn, and a time to dance
(Ecclesiastes 3:1, 4).

Missionaries experience the whole gamut of emotions during their careers. From the pen and wisdom of King Solomon once more we borrow headings to illustrate our experience. This one has to do with a *TIME TO LAUGH*, although at the time, the incident could have been anything but funny.

A good Filipino friend and respected evangelist came to the clinic one morning, complaining of a sore throat. That was early in our work in Malaybalay. The Essons[1], Ron and Davie, were getting used to working with us in the original dispensary building on the edge of the mission compound. The medical staff was composed of Ron as pharmacist, Davie and my wife Lenore as nurses, and me as physician. Two Filipino women, Carmen and Tining, were our clinic assistants and translators whenever needed. They proved to be indispensable.

The clinic was a simple wood-frame building elevated three feet off the ground on hardwood posts. The four-inch-thick thatch roof was rain-proof. Prior to World War II, the building had been used as a dispensary by ABWE missionary nurses: Rhoda Little, Gladys DeVries and Jeanne Wagner (who later became Mrs. Humbert Tentarelli).[2] They were well trained and respected practitioners,

[1] Appendix A
[2] Ibid

known throughout the province of Bukidnon. But when we arrived, they were all on assignments in the USA.

The clinic was partitioned off into four small rooms, one of which was my examining room. It had the basic furnishings: a table for the patient, a chair, and a stool. One wall had a built-in cabinet, on the shelves of which were instruments, bandages, and other supplies. Among these were some pint-sized open glass jars stuffed with various supplies. The wooden tongue blades were within reach behind me as I faced the patient on the table.

This was the scene as evangelist Libertad sat before me, complaining of a sore throat. Obviously, to examine the throat properly, the doctor needs adequate light and a tongue depressor. I gave Lenore the flashlight to aim into the patient's mouth, now widely opened. Since I knew the position of the commonly used items in the cabinet, it took only a brief glance to pull a tongue blade from its jar and place it on Pastor Libertad's tongue in one smooth motion.

Parenthetically, I should explain that in medical school, students are taught to develop an unflappable demeanor so that they appear calm regardless of what may come as a surprise. In that way the patient is not unnecessarily alarmed.

Pastor Libertad was seated before me with head extended, eyes closed, mouth open, and a blade pressing down on his tongue. To my chagrin, what did I see standing on the very tip of that tongue blade with tentacles fanning the back of his throat? A huge cockroach, at least two inches in length, poised to fly. I do not believe I had ever seen an insect that size, staring back at me with twitching antennae and beady red eyes.

With as controlled a tone as possible, I admonished the pastor, "Now, do not breathe and do not move, Brother Libertad."

Keeping his head steady and eyes closed, the pastor behaved perfectly while I flicked the insect onto the floor and reinserted the now empty blade for the inspection. In this emergent situation, it didn't occur to me to switch to a new blade. Anyway, austerity was our policy.

To this day, I have my *what if* thoughts. What if the pastor had gagged or inhaled deeply? What if the cockroach had decided to escape in one direction or another? What if Lenore and/or I had given vent to our inner emotions and yelled — or fainted? To my knowledge, the patient has remained unaware of our encounter with that unwelcome cockroach. Furthermore, he happily recovered from his ailment. The next time I heard him preach, the pastor's voice was normal.

A TIME TO GIVE BIRTH

I wrote about the birth of our first-born, Linda, during our days in the Navy at Sangley Point, Cavite. Eventually, we assisted in a delivery almost every day after Bethel Baptist Hospital opened. Of course, some days there were none; other days there were many. But we averaged over 250 deliveries each year in Malaybalay.

The majority of nationals preferred home deliveries with midwives who sent us the problem patients they couldn't deliver. So the number of deliveries by forceps or Cesarean section were relatively higher than we would have expected. Nevertheless, that did save lives of both mothers and babies. For the most part, the obstetrical ward was a happy place. Everyone loves a newborn.

We delivered many missionary babies, among whom were Sandra and Shirley, our own daughters. Not every father has the privilege of delivering his own children. However, it seemed that most of the MK's (missionary kids) were born to parents from the nearby Wycliffe Bible Translators' base in Nasuli, 15 miles (24 kilometers) south of Malaybalay. As if to advertise that fact, the translators gave our ABWE hospital a new meaning for its acronym: the Association of Baptists for Wycliffe Enlargement!

Some of the ABWE missionaries came from great distances to have their babies delivered at our facility in Malaybalay. A guest apartment was provided while they awaited the birth. Among them was the Ebersole family. Russ and Gene were busily engaged in a church planting ministry in Bacolod City at the time their baby was due to make her entrance into the world. In February 1955 the family came down a few weeks ahead of the expected date. Since this was their second child, Russ and Gene were quite relaxed about the whole thing.

Gene Ebersole was quite at home in Malaybalay. She was an MK herself, born to Henry and Gladys DeVries[3]. Her parents had been pioneer missionaries with a Dutch Reformed mission in Mindanao during the mid-1920's. Later, they resigned that mission group and aligned with ABWE. Their headquarters had been in Malaybalay. In 1926 Gene was born in the coastal city of Cagayan de Oro, where hospital facilities were more adequate. The city was 75 miles (120 kilometers) to the north, up the dusty and bumpy highway.

Gene grew up in Malaybalay. But when the Japanese army invaded Mindanao in 1942 the DeVries family was interned in the notorious Japanese prison camps. Their harrowing experiences during those four years of war have filled many books. The exciting finale came when they were rescued from the Los Baños camp south of Manila by the U.S. paratroopers in February 1945, one day before they all were to be executed.

After a period of recuperation in America following the war, Henry and Gladys returned to Malaybalay to rebuild and take up the work again. Their grown children remained behind in the States to pursue their education. At Wheaton College in Illinois, Gene met a young pre-seminary student, Russ Ebersole. It was love at first sight. Meanwhile, the senior DeVries stayed until retirement in the very house in which we now resided.

So Gene was actually "back home" when she and Russ came to Malaybalay in early 1955 to await the arrival of their baby. They enjoyed the accommodations of the guest apartment. We entertained them for some of their meals. At the supper table one evening the four of us were enjoying light chatter when I noted Gene's demeanor. "You'd better get downstairs, gal, real soon!" In those days the delivery room was on the ground floor of our residence.

That arrangement had its advantages and disadvantages. One advantage was that it took Lenore and Gene only a few seconds to get down to the ward adjacent to the delivery room and prepare for

[3] Appendix A

the imminent event. While the patient readied herself, the nurse prepared the next room for the delivery. Another advantage was that I could still keep track of the frequency of Gene's contractions even from upstairs. The flooring was not sufficiently insulated to make the labor room sound-proof.

Gene delivered her baby normally as I coached her along. Russ attentively supported Gene at the head of the table. Gasps of joy filled the room as their beautiful baby girl responded to my stimulating her first cry. They named her Cheri.

One of the chief disadvantages of the birthing facilities was that we could be awakened quite readily by the newborn's cry, since our bedroom was directly overhead. Nevertheless, in our experience of several hundreds, giving birth is usually a time of exhilaration and laughter! Stillbirths, neonatal problems and maternal emergencies were relatively rare.

AND A TIME TO DIE

In contrast to the joyful time surrounding a normal birth is the inevitable experience of having to deal with death. The occasion that comes to mind has the same "cast" in the same setting as the above scenario.

Again the four of us were at the table. It was in early 1964. By this time Cheri was nearly ten years old: the second oldest of the Ebersoles' five children. Now in their late thirties, Russ and Gene had come to Malaybalay because there was an unusual lump on Gene's chest. That afternoon I had taken her to the minor operating room in the new wing of Bethel Baptist Hospital, across the yard from our residence. The lump was removed under local anesthesia and the diagnosis was evident: recurrent cancer.

Gene had had a routine annual physical examination in the city of Iloilo four years prior to this. At that time, Dr. Daehler, an American physician in the Iloilo Mission Hospital, had felt a tiny hard mass in Gene's right breast and advised a biopsy. That proved to be an early cancer. The Ebersoles asked that I be advised by telegram, requesting that I come to Iloilo and perform the surgery. I did this and the radical mastectomy had been without complications. There was no evidence of spread to the lymph glands. We were all relieved and confident that she would fully recover.

Back then, there were no oncologists to consider chemotherapy, and radiation treatment was not a good option, considering the rather primitive equipment available. Gene made a smooth recovery and after a week was back home with her happy and growing family.

Now here we were four years later. A recurrence of the cancer, with involvement of deep nodes beneath the sternum, is notoriously ominous, carrying a poor prognosis. The four of us were rather somber as we sat about the supper table.

"Well, what do you recommend for us now, Link?" Russ's question was not unexpected.

Having thought through the prognosis which Gene would probably be experiencing, I replied, "I think your family should take an emergency medical furlough as soon as you can get your business responsibilities in order. You'll want to spend the Thanksgiving holiday with your folks back home." As soon as they could make arrangements, the Ebersoles flew to America.

Surrounded by her family, our dear friend Gene died on Thanksgiving Day, 1964, enabling her to praise and thank her Lord face to face. She was 38 years old.

Russ wrote us in February, 1965:

> "Surely, your prayers have meant much to us during these lonely days! Please continue to bear us up before our God, who alone can give real comfort and peace. At times it just doesn't seem real that our beloved has gone; at other times the reality of her absence is so gripping it is almost overwhelming! I feel so utterly incomplete without her for she was everything to me, as you well know. But the Lord wanted her and her ministry must have been finished on earth. Humanly speaking, this is difficult to understand when one considers her age, our children, our ministry together, etc. 'His ways are higher than

our ways, and His thoughts than our thoughts.'

Yes, how well I remember the many, many happy times the four of us have had. How pleased Geney was when we could get together. Just last week we celebrated Cheri's tenth birthday and I told her of the night she was born. Do you remember? The four of us were having dinner in your home and were just finishing dessert when you looked at Gene and said, 'You'd better get downstairs, gal, real soon.' And little Cheri appeared within an hour."

Not all deaths are sad occasions. That sounds odd, doesn't it? But it is true. We have actually been spiritually refreshed by the attitude and behavior of relatives of some of our dying patients. Upon other occasions we have been made miserable with the mourning and grieving of the bereaved whose conduct points up their hopelessness.

So, what makes the difference? Why do some people fall apart in their grief while others accept it more calmly? By that I do not mean that the latter are not grieving; rather, they are accepting the loss as a divine appointment as Russ did. The Bible ascribes such behavior as appropriate for those "who grieve, but not as others who have *no hope.*" The key is in the word *hope.* That passage of scripture goes on to read:

> For if we believe that Jesus died and rose again, even so them also which sleep in Jesus will God bring with Him ... For the Lord Himself shall descend from heaven with a shout, with the voice of the archangel, and with the trump of God: and the dead *in Christ* shall rise first: then we which are alive and remain shall be caught up together with them in the clouds, to meet the Lord in the air: and so shall we ever be with the Lord. Wherefore comfort one another with these words (1 Thessalonians 4:14, 16-18).

Which brings us to the reason for having mission hospitals and clinics in the first place. Such institutions are not to be simply social agencies concerned for the physically afflicted. Rather, a clinic or hospital worthy of the designation of "Christian" must be involved with the whole person: body, soul and spirit. Treating only the physical aspect is incomplete care. That is solely an exercise in postponing the inevitable: physical death. The goal of each of our mission medical teams must be to introduce our patients to the Great Physician, Jesus Christ, who alone gives *eternal* life to the soul who is willing to trust Him.

With this goal in mind, we placed over the door of Bethel Baptist Hospital a motto, taken from Mark 8:36-37:

> For what shall it profit a man, if he shall gain the whole world [*including a healthy body*], and lose his own soul?
> Or what shall a man give in exchange for his soul?

As King Solomon wrote, "There is an appointed time for everything... a time to give birth, and a time to die...." Wise men and women today will be prepared.

8

A TIME TO PLANT

"To everything there is a season,
and a time to every purpose under heaven...
a time to plant, and a time to pluck up that which is planted"
(Ecclesiastes 3:1-2).

Farming is not for sissies: especially rice farming. We had never observed rice farming before going to the tropics, where rice is the primary crop. Filipinos sing a song to a lilting tune that describes what hard work it is. One verse goes like this:

"Planting rice is never fun,
Bent from dawn to set of sun:
Cannot stand, and cannot sit;
Cannot rest for a little bit!"

Not only is planting hard work; it requires teamwork. Many farmers work together to sow and reap. Harvest time seems to require the most urgency, and it is the happiest time for the laborers. That's when they get paid.

Missionary work requires teamwork, also. Upon our arrival in Malaybalay in April 1952, we were eager to get acquainted with our neighbors with whom we would be "sowing and reaping," in the spiritual metaphor. That wasn't at all difficult. Lenore and I found we were enriched with colleagues, both missionaries and nationals, establishing life-long ties.

The house on the Bethel Baptist Hospital compound that had been designated for our use reminded me of my uncle's summer cottages on the shore of Lake Erie back in New York state. Our house in Malaybalay had two stories: the residence upstairs, and a car-port and storage area on the ground floor. The walls and partitions upstairs were single-sided; the studs were exposed on the inside walls. We learned that was to prevent *rats* from building their nests in the spaces which are created by having double-walls. Who wants to provide housing for the rodent population? The building was constructed totally of wood. The beams and flooring were Philippine mahogany, which comes in several varieties. These hardwoods are the most resistant to termites. So *now* the implication was that we would be dealing with both rats *and* termites.

What we especially appreciated was the spaciousness. Three bedrooms surrounded a large living-dining room combination. The kitchen and pantry were adjacent to the dining room. A bathroom separated two of the bedrooms. The walls throughout were unpainted, as was the outside of the house. The inside walls of the living room were made of horizontal tongue-andgroove boards, each six inches wide and a half inch thick.

We would learn to refer to the living room as the *sala*, pronounced with the broad Spanish vowel sounds (sah-lah) with a little stress on the first syllable. Since the same word with stress on the second syllable means "sin", we had to be precise in pronunciation. The room opened its full width onto the screened balcony, from which it was separated by four fan-folded doors. When these were closed to keep out the weather, the only light came through windows at the other end of the room. On a gloomy day, this arrangement gave me the distinct feeling of being crated. When we had finally settled into our quarters, however, Lenore saw to it that our home was tastefully decorated.

Harmonious relationship with our neighbors was not dependent upon us all being of the same even temperament. Nor did we come from similar ethnic or social backgrounds. Far from it. The cement that bonded us was the *team* relationship. Some were specialists in youth ministries, others in pastoral areas of responsibility, still others were outreach evangelists. The medical part of the team fits best into the latter category. The mission clinics and hospitals are outreaches of the church into the communities.

A better analogy of such a working relationship is the one found in Paul's first letter to the Christians in Corinth:

> For as the *body* is one, and hath many members, and all the members of that one body, being many, are one body: so also is Christ (1 Corinthians 12:12).

As we worked side by side with the others on our team, we learned their strengths and weaknesses, their likes and dislikes. Each person is unique. It seems that the individual's true colors show up best against the black-velvet background of *stress:* pain, grief and exhaustion. Stress enters into everyone's experience at some time or other. The scriptures remind us that gold and silver come from the refiner's fire; the perfect ceramic vessel results from the pressure of the potter's hands on the soft clay as he spins the wheel.

When missionaries, then, live in close proximity and work together in the same confines day-in and day-out, stress is bound to occur. Therefore, we counsel missionary appointees to the Philippines to bear that in mind before moving onto a mission compound. If they have a choice — realizing this will not be possible in every country — missionaries should choose a residence that is a little distance from the colleagues with whom they will be working every day. In this way, they will be able to get away for a sufficient period each day, in their own homes. Rather than bunch mission houses on the same acre of land, missionaries should consider renting adequate quarters in the village on a par with nationals who are teachers or government employees. By doing this, they might avoid being considered too American, or too ostentatious, and their neighbors will feel more comfortable dropping in for a visit.

When we arrived in the Philippines, we lived on the edge of a town with a population of around ten thousand people. The mission owned about four acres of land with three buildings as missionary residences. The decision was made for us. We moved into the house recently vacated by missionaries on furlough. Our immediate neighbors were ABWE missionaries. Let me introduce them to you.

ALFRED AND RUTH CONANT[1] arrived in Bukidnon in 1950. They occupied the house directly across the lawn from ours. Their two children, Joy and John, became close friends with our two oldest. Al was a seminary graduate and had been a chaplain in the U. S. Army during the war with Japan. Part of his military duty had been in the Philippines, which influenced his decision as to where he and Ruth would serve as missionaries after returning to civilian life and an interim pastorate in Hackensack, New Jersey.

At the time of our arrival, Al was pastor of Bethel Baptist Church. He had only a fifty yard walk to the chapel, since it was on the front edge of the mission property. He was an excellent preacher and Bible teacher, well loved by the members of the congregation. Ruth was the faithful pastor's wife, gifted as a secretary and pianist. The abilities of one complemented those of the other — an effective God-made match.

But Al was also an evangelist at heart and was restless unless he was reaching out to unevangelized areas. In early 1952 he and Ron Esson made a survey of Davao province, 200 miles (320 kilometers) to the south, at the request of national believers. The challenge was so great that Al later led a gospel team of Filipino pastors and evangelists there for a major campaign during May and June of that year. The Conant family subsequently moved to the small city of Tagum to spear-head the advance of the gospel in Davao province.

Before the Conants moved to Davao, Al underwent the routine physical and laboratory examinations that we advise our missionaries to have annually. Al was harboring a parasite that responds to a medicine called atabrine, which was also effective in treating malaria years ago. The regimen for Al's condition, however, required a prolonged course of the treatment. One of the side-effects, as veterans of the war in the Pacific may recall, is that the skin temporarily turns yellow while the patient is taking the medicine. But another rarer complication arose in Al's case: transient cerebral symptoms, producing irrational behavior. The first symptom of this developed as he was driving home from a weekend of meetings in another town. Fortunately, Al had a companion with him in the car, Mr. Artymiak.

[1] Appendix A

He was an interesting person, a "white Russian" as distinct from the Communist "reds." He had escaped from Russia and immigrated to the Philippines some years before and was now living with his family in Davao. His expertise was in tuning pianos. Since Conants owned an instrument, he periodically visited them and had established a cordial friendship.

Mr. Artymiak had met Al somewhere along the way and was now a passenger on the return trip to Tagum. Al suddenly felt faint but had presence of mind enough to pull off the dirt road and stop. Mr. Artymiak immediately provided treatment with a whiff or two of spirits of ammonia plus a tablet of digitalis, and took over the driving. They sped to Tagum and the Conant's house.

By this time Al was shouting and carrying on irrationally. As he entered the house, the usually sedate Reverend Conant shouted from the balcony, "TAGUM, REPENT!" Apparently, he was ready to deliver a forceful fire-and-brimstone sermon. He was hurried inside and placed on his bed. At that moment, his good friend, a Filipino minister, rushed in to see what was going on. Upon seeing him, the patient leaped from his bed and embraced the frightened pastor with such fervor that both landed in a heap on the floor.

Several friends were required to restrain Al sufficiently to get him back into another vehicle and speed off to the hospital in Davao City, about 40 minutes away. The emergency staff there sedated Al and gave him intravenous fluids. Meanwhile, Ruth notified me by telegram about the hospitalization. I wired back, "STOP THE ATABRINE!" The atabrine effect gradually wore off and he returned to his senses. He returned home with aching muscles from the struggle, but in his right mind. Al never took atabrine again.

Some months later when we had occasion to be with them, we asked Ruth what went through her mind. She replied, "All I could think was, 'Our missionary career is over. I'll just have to institutionalize Alfred!'"

How grateful we were that this was not the case. They went on to make an impressive impact upon that province with several churches established and Filipino pastors trained to take over this ministry. ABWE missionaries have been actively involved in Davao province ever since.

As for the Conants, they later took on a new challenge in Baguio City, located in the mountains of northern Luzon. Al had been instrumental in starting a small Baptist church there while still in the military service shortly after the Japanese surrendered in World War II. Leadership was needed for further growth of the work in the Baguio area, and no one was better qualified than were the Conants. Even though Alfred was plagued with health problems, the Conants spent many productive years in the Philippines. Upon retirement, they found comfortable accommodations in Florida. Al went to be with the Lord a few years later; Ruth now lives near her daughter in Tennessee.

"THE AUNTIES" was the label given to Priscilla Bailey and Mildred Crouch[2]. No one mentions their names without smiling. Anecdotes involving them are endless — and humorous. For one thing, their accent betrayed that they came from New England — the Boston area, to be exact. You can imagine how that complicated their ability to learn a foreign language. They just couldn't pronounce their "R's" with the distinctive quality given that consonant in Philippine dialects.

They, too, were in Malaybalay when we arrived, having preceded us by about three months. Had they not been there, we wonder how we could have raised our five children.

These two met in Providence Bible Institute in Rhode Island. They had a lot in common and became close friends throughout the academic years. Both knew that they wanted to be missionaries in some foreign country. When it came time to join a mission agency, they both applied to ABWE and were accepted. The mission board appointed them to work in the Philippines. Since they proved they could work harmoniously together while in training, they were assigned as youth workers to the Bukidnon team.

Their first responsibility was supervising a boarding house for high school girls in Malaybalay. These girls came from homes of Baptist church members who wanted their daughters to stay in the

[2] Appendix A

ABWE dormitory. The dorm needed someone as supervisor, so when these two Bostonians arrived, their colleagues felt they were the answer. This proved to be ideal, indeed. The "Aunties" had living quarters in the dorm building, located at the rear of the mission compound. Most boarders could return home over the weekends, so the missionaries took on teaching opportunities as well.

Millie and Priscilla were experts in setting up Sunday schools and developing teaching material for churches in the area. Furthermore, they were involved in training teachers for these courses. This was done primarily during the two-week Short-Term Bible Institutes[3] held for pastors and workers about three times each year. The missionary men taught classes for the pastors and the "Aunties" taught pastors' wives and other ladies who were eager to upgrade their work with children. Usually an out-of-town guest speaker was invited to deliver a deeper-life inspirational message to the whole group each morning and to preach an evangelistic sermon each evening. Everyone in the host village was invited to attend the evening sessions.

Those short-term institutes were the only formal Bible training that some of the provincial pastors and leaders could obtain. The expense of leaving their villages to take a three-year course at a more elaborate Bible school in a distant city was not practical. The men who were the best qualified to be church leaders were married and had to support their families.

So the local churches in the province (which numbered about 20 in the 1950's) took turns hosting the institutes. The members of those churches provided places for their guests to sleep and took the responsibility of cooking the meals. Usually the dining area was under the shelter of a tent. Those who attended paid a small tuition for the lesson materials and a fee for their room and board.

During those early years, the clinic work was not too heavy and did not keep the medical team from helping with the Bible institutes. Ron and I looked forward to being members of the faculty. Our wives seldom could attend, however, because of the children, but if the host church was close enough to Malaybalay, they attended the

[3] Appendix D

77

evening services. But those meetings often took us away for a week or so at a time. Almost invariably, it seemed, one of our own children would get sick in our absence. Linda, for instance, came down with a roaring case of measles on one such occasion.

Sometimes the host church was in a mountain village, which could be reached only after several hours' hike from our town. We soon found that our Filipino friends could out-hike us and seemed to thrive on the vigorous exercise required. It didn't seem to matter how distant the church might be. Sometimes the people attending rode for hours on a bus, then hiked through rivers, over muddy trails and across mountains just to get there.

The missionaries were assigned to one of the houses in the village which had been vacated for the occasion. With both men and women in the team, it was often necessary to partition off sleeping quarters. For beds we unrolled sleeping bags or inflated air mattresses and arranged them on the split-bamboo floor. We always slept under mosquito nets to keep out whatever pests might be flying or crawling about. On some of those excursions we brought along our own food supplies. We men were especially grateful when the women were along to take charge of cooking on the crude wood-burning stoves.

After several years of these short-term Bible institutes, we noticed that the most promising young men and women needed the more formal environment of a regular Bible school. Furthermore, such a school would best serve the needs of the province if it was kept in the provincial setting rather than sending the students to city campuses. Besides, some of the graduates of the urban schools were reluctant to return to the simpler life and smaller churches in the province.

So the Bukidnon Association of Baptist Churches (BABC[4]), in consultation with the ABWE church-planters, thought it wise to have a regional Bible Institute. Pastor Antonio Ormeo, Rev. Earl Carlberg, Pastor Norberto Selorio and the Aunties were among the people God used to start a school in Bukidnon in 1956.

At first the school was held in Bethel Baptist Church, located on the front of the mission property. Before long the school moved further into the town of Malaybalay where the church had built a new and

[4] Appendix B

78

larger sanctuary. As the school grew, so did the need for larger facilities. Property was donated near the Wycliffe base in Nasuli, Bukidnon and today the Mindanao Baptist Bible Institute[5] is training men and women for leadership in the provincial churches. In Bukidnon alone, those Baptist churches now number over 200.

The team of Bailey-'n'-Crouch made their most indelible contribution to church growth in their work with children. They not only taught others how to teach in Sunday schools and junior church settings, but they demonstrated the vital necessity of loving kids in the process. They promoted children's activities throughout the week. Sometimes that would be impromptu sessions of play finishing with a Bible story. Neighborhood JOY Clubs sprang up through their inspiration. These resulted in unchurched kids becoming interested in the Bible and then in attending Sunday schools.

But what we missionary parents especially appreciated was the loving way these Aunties spent time with our own kids, skillfully nurturing them in the Lord in the process. And they weren't push-overs when it came to discipline. Our children grew up respecting adults and authority figures, though that was sometimes a painful process.

One time a number of visiting missionary families arrived on the mission compound for a field council session. When the adults were busy with meetings, the kids were having a grand time with their peers. But Millie saw from her vantage point across the yard that our son Dave, at the tender age of about five years, had opened a second floor window of our house and was leaning out precariously.

So she left the meeting and called out in firm tones, "David, get back from that window and close it before you fall!"

Dave recognized the voice of authority and was about to retract from his position when one of his visiting little friends behind him remarked, "She's not your mother. You don't have to obey her!"

Apparently, that was a new idea. It put a spark of fire in his brain, and it did seem to make sense. He decided to put the theory to the test. He shouted back from the still open window, "I don't have to obey you. *You* aren't my mother!"

[5] Appendix E

Imagine his startled reaction when he saw Aunt Millie drop what she was doing, race across the yard and start climbing our back steps. His eyes opened wide, his jaw dropped, and his little counselors disappeared from the scene. The house rattled as his Auntie pounded up the back stairs. He had no place to hide. The two of them had a loving chat followed by the appropriate application of the board of education to his seat of learning. A few more minutes of soothing hugs and reconciliation closed the lesson.

Dave carried that practical laboratory experiment in his memory from that day forward. Of course back then neither of them could anticipate that before their careers ended many years later, Dave would become the ABWE Coordinator for the Philippine Field Council, and Millie and Priscilla would proudly submit to his leadership.

After two terms of service in Bukidnon, the Aunties felt that their expertise in helping organize new churches with structured Sunday schools and youth groups should be put to a new challenge that was opened to them on the island of Leyte. In 1961 they transferred to the town of Hilongos, on the western coast of Leyte, to join Larry and Jacqui Armstrong. Their faithfulness in this new team effort resulted in the establishing of at least two new churches there.

Besides that, they were instrumental in the development of *Leyte Baptist Clinic & Hospital*[6].

9
A TIME TO BUILD UP

"To everything there is a season,
and a time to every purpose under heaven:
... a time to break down, and a time to build up" (Ecclesiastes 3:1,3).

RON AND LAURA (DAVIE) ESSON[1] arrived in Malaybalay in the autumn of 1951, about six months before we got there. They had applied to ABWE specifically to be part of the medical team. Ron was a pharmacist and Davie (short for Davidson, her maiden name) was a nurse. No one ever called her by the name Laura, it seemed. Their two sons, Shan and Dick became close friends with the other MK's (missionary kids) in the area, and we adults took on the role of "aunties" and "uncles" — a common practice with mission families around the world.

The reason for this custom is that our relationships often were closer with our fellow missionaries and our Christian friends than with our biological extended families. A statement Jesus made implies the same sentiment:

Verily I say unto you, There is no man that hath left house, or brethren, or sisters, or father, or mother, or wife, or children, or lands, for my sake, and the gospel's, but he shall receive an hundredfold now in this time, houses, and brethren, and sisters, and mothers, and children, and lands, with persecutions; and in the world to come eternal life (Mark 10:29-30).

The Essons remain that kind of family to us. As the familiar chorus says, "*I'm so glad I'm a part of the family of God!*" (William

[1] Appendix A

81

J. and Gloria Gaither).

Ron and Davie took over the clinic that the missionary nurses had started earlier. Soon it was officially named the Bethel Baptist Clinic. Ron not only contributed his expertise in setting up a suitable pharmacy in the dispensary building, but he also saw to it that the clinic could do some of the essential laboratory tests. Furthermore, he became adept at extracting the bad teeth of suffering dental patients. He learned this skill along with a class of medical students in special sessions at White Memorial Hospital in Los Angeles, where he also acquired proficiency in doing basic laboratory techniques prior to coming to the mission field.

To prove that a missionary must be adaptable, Ron also became my anesthetist when we began to do major surgery. He had to become familiar with the anesthetic that was available at the time: ether. It came in cans which were sealed with a special metal top. The anesthetist would pierce the lid of the can with a safety pin and then drip the ether on a face-mask held over the patient's nose and mouth. To this day, the smell of ether gives me flash-backs to the time when I had my own tonsils removed. The induction and recovery phases of being anesthetized with ether linger still in my memory. Anesthetics today are so much better in comparison.

I well remember one of our first surgery patients — a dainty little Filipina named Molly, with acute appendicitis. She became ill one day with a severe stomach ache. Her mother brought her in for a check-up, and the diagnosis was unmistakable. We got the surgical room ready, placed her on the table and Ron began the ether drip.

The procedure went smoothly, and I removed the offending appendix. As I began to close the wound, I told Ron he should stop the anesthetic so that, by the time I finished, the patient would begin to awaken. The last of the stitches was in when Ron recognized that little Molly was about to vomit, another common sequel to ether anesthesia (as I can attest from my personal experience). He turned her head to the side and readied the basin.

But then we all felt equally nauseated when Ron exclaimed, "Look! What's this coming out her nose?"

We soon learned that most, if not all of our pediatric patients, have intestinal parasites — worms. In diagnosing and treating children, we decided from then on to look for evidence of parasites and treat that as well as the major ailment. At the operating table we proved that ether disturbs and numbs more than the patient; the worms don't like it either.

Molly recovered smoothly and became a close friend of our blond three-year-old daughter, Linda. They were the same size, build, and temperament — a delightful picture in black-and-white as they played together. Of course, Molly received the proper treatment for the parasites, but we knew she would have an on-going battle to remain free of such "critters."

To prove my point, the elementary school in town conducted a contest once or twice each year as part of its instruction in hygiene. The rural health officer provided the teachers with medicine to rid the students of worms. Then the various classrooms vied for first place to see which group of kids could bring in the most *ascaris* (worms). They didn't necessarily count each worm. They counted the filled jars.

Repulsive? Probably so: but it caused me to wonder how our heavenly Father must feel when He looks at *us* sin-laden creatures. "Man looketh on the outward appearance, but the Lord looketh on the heart" (1 Samuel 16:7). Oh, we may try to clean things up, but then we return to our old habits and come up with the same old results. What those school children needed was a permanent cure followed by a new life-style. And that is what we mortals need when it comes to dealing with our sin problem.

> There is none righteous, no, not one; ... For all have sinned, and come short of the glory of God" (Romans 3:10,23).

But thank God, there *is* a permanent cure for the sin-problem:

> For the wages of sin is death; but the gift of God is eternal life through Jesus Christ our Lord (Romans 6:23).

Furthermore, there is a solution to the problem of the daily contamination that comes with living in this evil world of ours after we have received this gift from God, for:

If we walk in the light, as he is in the light, we have fellowship one with another, and the blood of Jesus Christ his Son cleanseth us from all sin. If we say we have no sin, we deceive ourselves, and the truth is not in us. If we confess our sins, he is faithful and just to forgive us our sins, and to cleanse us from all unrighteousness (1 John 1:7-9).

Ron and Davie were good neighbors and great to have on the team. Davie and Lenore worked well together. In early 1953, they even discovered that they were both "in the family way." Their expected due dates were within a couple of weeks of each other. They worked along together and compared notes on their progress. Excitement rose as the dates grew nearer.

Since both of these nurses were indispensable in the operating room, I was concerned that they should not get overly stressed during their pregnancies. You wouldn't label either of them as being squeamish, exactly, but as time went along, I noted some changes. For instance, one of them would be in the surgery as my assistant while the other would be the circulating nurse. They took turns, since one job was perhaps more interesting than the other.

Upon more than one occasion, while we were in the middle of an operation, my assisting nurse would declare that she felt light-headed and might faint. Immediately, the other would scrub up and take her place, only to spend a few minutes and state that now *she* felt faint. They switched back and forth throughout the procedure, being careful to maintain sterility — in the surgical meaning of the term, of course. With both husbands also at work in the room, we were able to empathize with them and not to become rattled by these distractions.

Finally, the dates of delivery were upon us in the autumn of 1953. The darling baby girls were born about two weeks apart: Susie to the Essons and Sandy to us Nelsons. Since we had set up temporary rooms for surgical and obstetrical patients on the ground floor of our residence at that time, these girls, to this day, tell their friends that they were born under our house. We all enjoyed observing their growth and development. They were like sisters in so many ways throughout their early childhood — and even to this day.

Dull moments were rare. Our two families were involved in everything together: the clinic, the church, and social activities. Ron and I were especially busy during evangelistic campaigns and the short-term Bible Institutes[1]. I wrote a letter to our parents in January 1954:

> "This week Ron and I have been at the tent campaign every night but Saturday. This was Ron's week to preach, leaving me as the song-leader and operator of the projector for the colored slides depicting the life of Christ. We can always be assured of a good hearing if we hold out the bait of a slide show after the message. Next week will be my turn again to preach, while Ron is the prop man. We are presenting the Word of God systematically. We trust that the Lord will work through His Word and, in spite of the tools He is using, win many souls from darkness into His wondrous light. Two more weeks will follow. One of our missionaries is coming from Manila as a guest speaker and teacher at the Bible Institute."

Two weeks later as the campaign was winding down, I wrote another follow-up letter which reported the results.

> "This evening we start the last two weeks at Linabo. We know you are praying. Friday evening for the first time there was unashamed response to the invitation and seven young people (five men and two ladies) came forward and seemed most earnestly to accept the Lord. This is only the beginning, we trust, of a real awakening in that *barrio* (village) that has hitherto been so hardened to the gospel. Continue to pray for these two weeks are the most important. The Chiltons (our guests from Manila) are a real attraction with their music. The pastors and leaders from our churches will all be gathering, and the two week institute will make a fine climax to the campaign.

[1] Appendix D

House-to-house visitation is on the schedule. PRAY!"

The Essons had a variety of assignments on the ABWE team. In 1961 when they returned from a regular furlough, Ron and Davie agreed to become dormitory parents for the ABWE missionary kids attending high school in Baguio City, about 650 miles (1000 kilometers) north of Malaybalay. This occupied much of their third term of missionary service. The role of dorm parents is a vital one for the missionary families, since it is always heart-wrenching to have to send the youngsters that far away for high school. But with dependable folks like the Essons acting as proxy parents to children from other families, the separation was more bearable. Ron became involved in the church-planting ministry of ABWE in that city as well.

In 1964 Ron went on another survey trip. This time it was to the islands of the Palawan chain on the far western side of the Philippines. The regional ABWE field council requested that he join them to determine the feasibility of having a mission hospital there, similar to the one in Mindanao. Their report was positive. Consequently, the Essons received an invitation to join in the medical outreach prior to the actual construction of a building. The Essons continued in Palawan until 1973. During their time there, they requested the help of Missionary Aviation Fellowship to fly the team into some of the more remote areas.

Ron and Davie set up an itinerary of monthly fly-in clinics. They flew into remote coastal villages to examine and treat indigent patients. In the evenings they held gospel services. Then the next day flew on to another village to repeat the agenda. In 1971 an ABWE doctor, Jim Entner[2], and his wife Esther finished their Tagalog language study and began their first term in Palawan. Jim joined the Essons in the medical work. Esther's forte was working with youth and counseling. They not only met medical and dental needs, but groups of believers sprang up. Churches formed and the Baptist fellowship grew.

This response convinced the field council to build a hospital in Roxas, a small town on the northeast coast of the island. ABWE missionary Bud DeVries and his crew of men faithfully labored

[2] Appendix A

through the construction period. In June 1977 the Palawan Baptist Hospital was dedicated to the Lord, and opened for business. Eventually, ABWE pilots Larry Holman and Harry Rogers joined the team and brought a Cessna-180 plane to Roxas as a base for the flight program[3].

THE LEYTE BAPTIST CLINIC & HOSPITAL

Recognizing the expertise of Ron and Davie Esson in developing medical outreaches, another ABWE field council (composed of the Larry Armstrongs, the Jim Ankneys and Priscilla Bailey and Millie Crouch) asked for their services to start a similar ministry on the island of Leyte, on the far eastern side of the country. By early 1973 a second ABWE doctor, Phil Young, and his family had arrived to work in Palawan. The Essons considered that as the timing of the Lord and transferred to Hilongos, Leyte. Here the ABWE church-planters had rented housing and were reaching out with evangelistic meetings in the area. Regular church services were begun in their youth center building in town. But opposition by leaders of the dominant religious group constantly hindered their work.

The field council reasoned that perhaps a medical team could help break down some of the prejudices that had created barriers to this Protestant movement. When the Essons accepted the challenge, they requested that a missionary doctor from Bethel Baptist Hospital in Malaybalay fly to Hilongos for one week each month and consider the potential for starting a hospital there. The plan worked out well. Lenore and I were flown there in the mission plane. Since the distance was about 155 air miles (250 kilometers), the trip took less than an hour. Much of the flight was over the open sea between islands — beautiful, but hazardous.

Whenever we arrived, a temporary clinic was ready. The medical team used two rooms in the youth center, located next to the elementary school. Patients came in increasing numbers and before long plans were drawn up for the construction of the Leyte Baptist Clinic and Hospital (LBC&H).

The problem was where to build; the local populous was reluctant to sell land to Baptists for any purpose. In 1961 when Millie Crouch and Priscilla Bailey arrived to help in church-planting with the Armstrongs, they were able to rent a suitable house only because the owners couldn't rent it or sell it to anyone else. That hacienda was reputed to be haunted. The father of the family who had lived there died, and his relatives insisted his ghost returned every night and knocked on the walls or caused other disturbance.

When Millie and Priscilla offered to rent that house, the family decided *that* might be a good way to scare the women away from town, so they consented. The "ghost" was no match for the faith of those missionaries and they lived there for several years. It was an attractive two story structure of Spanish architecture. Whenever they sat at their dining room table upstairs, they could look over the adjacent lot where a sugar-mill office was located. The building was of local frame materials: rattan and wood walls covered with a *cogon* grass thatch roof.

"If God would give us that property, our search for a hospital site would be over," they mused.

They did more: they prayed. Sometimes they prayed while walking around the entire four acre lot, claiming it for the Lord. But obtaining the property seemed hopeless. The proprietor was adamant: it was *not* for sale!

But God changed that owner's mind. A roaring fire burned down the entire office complex of the sugar mill. Of course, the ladies were not arsonists, but they *were* prayer warriors. God did the rest. Before long the proprietor reconsidered the offer that had been made previously. In 1974 the entire property was sold to the mission at a very reasonable price.

So the clinic building was constructed. The attractive cement block structure stands beside the main highway on the fringe of Hilongos. One corner of the area was selected as the church site with enough space for a parsonage behind. Two other residential lots farther back on the property were staked off for quarters for hospital personnel. Excitement rose as the buildings began to take shape. Leyte Baptist Clinic and Hospital became a reality and opened in 1975.

Experienced people came to set up different departments of the new hospital. Ron Esson prepared the pharmacy. Don Love,[4] an ABWE medical technologist, supervised the laboratory. Bill Stevenson, M.D., transferred from Malaybalay to be the first physician. Dr. Lualhati Gaspar, who specialized in obstetrics and gynecology, joined Bill. Barbara Love and Davie Esson were the supervising nurses, later joined for varying periods of time by nurses Barb Klumpp and Jan Whetstone. Qualified Christian Filipino nurses and technicians were hired for staff positions.

For the first two years the hospital was open, we Nelsons flew to Hilongos for a week of surgery each month. In 1979 the Essons left Leyte for their furlough to the USA. The Stevensons accepted the challenge to open a branch of Leyte Baptist Clinic in the town of Abuyog on the east coast. The medical committee invited us to move to Hilongos and head up the surgery department, sharing the increasing work load with Dr. Gaspar. We accepted and moved into the house vacated by the Stevensons on the hospital compound.

Now the routine was switched: from Leyte we flew back to Malaybalay one week each month. We cared for the major surgical problems of both hospitals. These hospitals were linked by short-wave radios. We kept daily radio contact with Jim and Esther Entner, who were then overseeing the work at Malaybalay. As capable Christian Filipino professionals were added, we gradually transferred responsibility from expatriates to nationals. In this way, Bethel Baptist Hospital in Malaybalay was the first of the ABWE medical facilities to become autonomous with an independent board of directors.

Dr. Ken Cole[5] and his family joined ABWE and arrived in Hilongos about 1977. His expertise was in pediatrics, which greatly enhanced the ability of LBC&H to meet the medical needs of that part of Leyte.

Now the medical-evangelistic program of the ABWE was in an expansion mode: first in Malaybalay, Bukidnon; then in Roxas, Palawan; and the third in Hilongos, Leyte. Most important of all, the hospitals were centers of evangelism. God was using medical teams as catalysts to introduce hundreds of people to Jesus Christ. Churches

[4] Appendix A
[5] Appendix A

increased in membership. New Baptist churches sprang up, adding to the fellowship of the Association of Fundamental Baptist Churches in the Philippines (AFBCP).

THE AKLAN BAPTIST HOSPITAL (ABH)[6]

The fourth and last of the ABWE hospitals in the Philippines is located in the village of Caticlan, in the municipality of Malay, Aklan on the northwest tip of the island of Panay. This small fishing community is about 150 miles (240 kilometers) northwest of Iloilo City. For many years Iloilo was the second largest city in the Philippines.

Iloilo City was the venue of the first missionaries of the Association of Baptists for Evangelism in the Orient (ABEO), later to be renamed the Association of Baptists for World Evangelism (ABWE). In 1928 Dr. Raphael C. Thomas arrived to be the team leader of the ABEO missionaries. Dr. Harold T. Commons, president of ABWE for 36 years, recorded the story in his book *Heritage & Harvest*:[7]

"Dr. Raphael C. Thomas was one of the old-time missionaries with a burden for souls. He was both an ordained minister and a medical doctor with degrees from Andover Newton Theological Seminary and the Harvard Medical College. He had been on the field approximately 25 years and was in charge of the Northern Baptist Mission hospital at Jaro, Iloilo. To him, medicine was not an end in itself, but a means to an end. Evangelism was his main burden. He loved to trek out into the countryside for a combination of medical and evangelistic work. This became a point of conflict when he was criticized by fellowworkers for not spending enough time in the hospital itself. Complaints were made against him to the mission board. Finally, an order came from the general secretary of the home board telling Dr. Thomas to cease his evangelistic itineration and confine himself

[6] Appendix K
[7] Harold T. Commons, D.D., *Heritage & Harvest; ABWE Insight Series, 1981, pages 5,6*

to running the hospital. This he could not conscientiously do. It was intolerable that he not be permitted to carry out his first love, evangelism, which was the primary reason for his presence on the field. He felt that he could not continue under that yoke.

Dr. Thomas and his family returned to the States on furlough early in 1927 and submitted his resignation. It was accepted. In the providence of God, if this had not happened, there might never have been an ABWE. As we look back, we say, 'Thank God for one man who had the courage to stand alone in loyalty to His Lord, to the Word of God, and to Christ's commission to go into all the world and preach the gospel to every creature.'"

Dr. Thomas had been among the first missionaries to arrive in the Philippines after the signing of the Treaty of Paris which ended the Spanish-American War in 1898. Speaking of that historic event, President William McKinley stated in one of his public addresses,

"I did not want the Philippine Islands and when we got them I did not know what to do with them. Often I fell on my knees before God to ask Him for guidance. Finally, late one night, it came to me this way. We had no choice in the matter. We had to take the governmental responsibility for the Philippines and then set ourselves to do three things: first of all, to civilize them; secondly, to educate them; and thirdly, to Christianize them and by God's grace to do everything we possibly could for them."[8]

Many of the major Protestant denominations responded to this concern of the U.S. president and sent missionaries to the Philippines. Among them were 25 mission agencies that sent out medical teams to start church-run hospitals throughout the archipelago. One of those was the Northern Baptist Convention. Doctor Thomas was one of the missionary physicians who helped establish the Baptist Mission Hospital in Iloilo City in 1902.

---

[8] *Victor Heiser, M.D. , An American Doctor's Odyssey; W.W.Norton & Co., Inc. 1936, page 10*

But 25 years later, in 1927, Dr. Raphael Thomas decided he could no longer work under the missionary society sponsoring that hospital. So in 1928 the Thomases and several other teachers at the Baptist college constituted the first missionaries of the new agency which eventually became the ABWE.

Now it was 1980 and ABWE was asked to consider taking on a fourth mission hospital in Aklan. This medical unit had a unique beginning. Chuck and Pauline Alianza of the Action International Ministries (AIM) had been missionaries in Malay, Aklan for about ten years. Their concern was especially for the aboriginal tribe of Ati located there. They not only actively evangelized among them, but Chuck was involved in translating the Bible into their own dialect. The Alianzas had also helped organize a local evangelical church on the edge of the town, to which both coastal Filipinos and interior Ati were welcome.

Pauline was increasingly in demand for medical help by the impoverished and sickly people of the area. Often the missionaries transported the more seriously ill over rough roads in all kinds of weather conditions to a hospital in the capital city of Kalibo. The one way trip took four hours if there were no obstructions along the way.

Feeling that something had to be done to make better medical assistance available, the Alianzas began searching for an answer. The AIM leadership did not feel that their organization should start a medical program of their own, though the need was evident. But neither would the mission hinder the Alianzas from finding an alternative. In their research, Chuck and Pauline visited the ABWE medical unit in Hilongos, Leyte. They saw what they felt was just what their hearts had desired: a small hospital with an evangelistic emphasis. They drew up plans, based on the blue-prints of Leyte Baptist Clinic & Hospital, and presented the project to both mission boards. In 1980 AIM agreed to sponsor the construction and ABWE agreed to administer the facility after it was built.

AIM purchased property bordering the landing-field of the small community airport. The Alianzas raised funds and stimulated interest among builders. A team of men came out from a supporting church in California to construct the hospital. AIM also supplied Filipino workers from their Manila project which taught young men a trade.

Early in 1982 the building was dedicated at a gala affair with dignitaries from the provincial medical society, politicians from the town, interested citizens and mission personnel.

Officials of both ABWE and AIM sent representatives. A plane of the JAARS (*Jungle Aviation and Radio Service*), a branch of Wycliffe, flew in personnel from Mindanao and Leyte.

Dr. Othello Caturan transferred from the Leyte Baptist Hospital to become the first resident physician of Aklan Baptist Hospital (ABH). He and his family sailed across the inter-island sea from Leyte in July 1982, and moved into rented quarters until their own staff house could be built at the rear of the hospital. Don and Barbara Love moved to ABH to set up the laboratory and business office. We Nelsons flew in from time to time to help with surgical consultations and to build Dr. Caturan's confidence in doing surgical procedures. With that beginning, the hospital became another monument to the grace of God.

I wonder if Dr. Thomas smiled down from heaven at the sight? His emphasis on evangelism remains the theme of each of the four ABWE hospitals in the Philippines. Each is administered by its own Board of Trustees and staffed by qualified Filipino medical and business personnel. The goal of each hospital continues to be quality medical care, lovingly rendered by dedicated Christian workers who openly proclaim Christ crucified, risen, and coming again.

10
A TIME TO WEEP, A TIME TO LAUGH

"To every thing there is a season ...
a time to weep, and a time to laugh"
(Ecclesiastes 3:1,4).

Which should I put first: the *weeping* or the *laughing*? At the time, the experiences were not funny; but neither were they disastrous. We rode on an emotional roller-coaster. Let me tell the events that occurred by first introducing the **STEVENSONS**. Bill won't mind.

A TIME TO WEEP

Bill Stevenson had a medical practice in the Haddon Heights area of New Jersey. He and his wife decided to become involved in medical-missionary work. But soon after they applied to serve with ABWE, tragedy struck. Bill's wife became ill with a rapidly growing cancer and died in 1966. In the course of his grieving, Bill felt that the Lord had not revoked his decision to enter missionary work, even though it meant doing so without his dear wife.

Preparation for missionary work with ABWE requires fund-raising. Before the 60's, it took about a year or so to raise the basic financial support. In more recent times it often takes two years or longer. That can be a difficult and discouraging task. Not everyone is a gifted speaker. Still, pre-field work is an important requirement of "faith-mission" agencies. The future missionary comes face to face with potential supporters. Without that backing, the "warrior" would be sent into battle without the essential supply line.

The apostle Paul stated the principle and set the example:
Whosoever shall call on the name of the Lord shall be
saved. How then shall they call on him in whom they
have not believed? And how shall they believe in him of
whom they have not heard? And how shall they hear
without a preacher? And *how shall they preach, except
they be sent?* (Romans 10:13-15).

Later, while on his missionary journey, Paul wrote to those who
were supporting him in the church at Philippi:
Ye have well done, that ye did communicate with my
affliction. Now ye Philippians know also, that in the
beginning of the gospel, when I departed from Macedonia,
no church communicated with me as concerning giving
and receiving, but ye only. Not because I desire a gift: but
I desire fruit that may abound to your account. But I have
all, and abound: I am full, having received of Epaphroditus
the things which were sent from you, an odor of a sweet
smell, a sacrifice acceptable, wellpleasing to God. But
my God shall supply all *your* need according to his riches
in glory by Christ Jesus (Philippians 4:14-19).

So Paul avows that both donor and recipient benefit from their
partnership in missionary ventures. The church that gives is blessed
— not just the missionary who receives. Faith-mission agencies
equate acquiring basic support with God's approval of that missionary
before he leaves his home soil.

A TIME TO LAUGH

Eventually Bill was cleared to leave the USA. He arrived in the
Philippines in the autumn of 1968 with three of his children: two
boys and a girl. The children enrolled in Faith Academy located on
the outskirts of Manila. That institution is one of the largest schools
for missionary children in the world. Bill's older twin boys, Bill and
John, and his older daughter, Sue, remained in the States to finish
their education.

The doctor entered a language school in Manila to learn Cebuano
Visayan and to become acquainted with the customs and culture of

Filipinos. Although this required hard work and intense concentration, the interaction with teachers and other students had hilarious moments. Americans have a knack for getting their tongues twisted. A good sense of humor helps immensely. You have to be able to laugh at yourself; others will.

When language study finally ended, the Stevenson family moved to Malaybalay and took up residence in the mission house across the yard from ours. Bill was soon involved in the hospital routines, sharing in the work load.

Imagine the reaction of his colleagues when Bill, the father of six children, announced that he was engaged to be married! What *must* his fiancee be like? We soon learned. Marilyn Tirrell was a widow whose pastor-husband had died in 1965, leaving her with four children. During a speaking engagement at the First Baptist Church of Tipton, Indiana in 1968, Bill had met Marilyn. It was love at first sight. When Bill left shortly thereafter for the Philippines, the flame of romance was fanned through correspondence. Meanwhile, Marilyn applied to ABWE and was also appointed as a missionary to the Philippines. By early autumn 1970, their plans were finalized. The wedding would be performed in Malaybalay. Most of their children would participate. Weather permitting, it would be held outdoors on the beautiful park-like grounds of the mission compound.

The Stevensons met Marilyn and her four children at the Manila International Airport. Then they all flew on the Philippine Airlines flight to Malaybalay for the festive occasion. October 24, 1970 dawned, beautiful and sunny. The bride was gorgeous; the groom handsome. The ceremony was conducted without a hitch, with joy and laughter. "And they lived happily ever after."

Well, I must modify that last statement considerably. The pendulum began to swing from the happy side, to the more serious. Times of laughter swung to serious moments.

A TIME TO WEEP

Let me set the stage for the next scene of the play. The *time*: February 1971, about three months after the beautiful wedding. The *place*: the Stevenson residence. The *cast*: the same people, plus another visitor, Roberta: wife of one of the Stevenson twins, John. She came to visit the newlyweds, and was expecting her first child. John had to finish his work at Faith Academy before he could join her.

I'll never forget the night when things began to happen over at Stevensons' house. We were alerted by a call from Marilyn on our field telephone. Have you ever seen those army field telephones? The compound buildings were linked by them. Each phone was powered by two flashlight batteries. A handle on the side of the case could be cranked to call someone on the line. Our number was one long ring; the next house, two rings; the hospital, one long, one short; and so it went around the campus.

Marilyn cranked out our ring. "Bill's sick; he's acting peculiar. Please come over!" Her voice betrayed an emergency and intense emotion.

I ran next door to their house and found Bill confused, slurring his speech, and unable to steady himself. We laboriously got him onto the sofa in the living room. He appeared to be having a stroke. Then he began to convulse, a moderately strong grand mal seizure. I sent for the medication which stops seizures and administered the first dose intravenously.

He relaxed. By this time, Lenore was comforting Marilyn. We soon learned that her distress was the more acute because her first husband had died during similar seizures. You can imagine her feelings. Just then Roberta waddled out of her room announcing, "I think the baby is coming!"

A TIME TO LAUGH, AGAIN

Talk about mixed emotions. "A time to laugh, and a time to weep." With Bill calmed down, we hurried Roberta to the hospital where Lenore and the duty nurse prepared for delivery.

The rest of the night I was on shifts: between the labor patient and the sick doctor. One thing is for certain: babies don't wait for anyone. Not even for a sick grandfather! Roberta made good progress and before many hours, the cry of the newborn rejoiced her mother's heart and brought a measure of reassurance to suffering grandparents. God was still in control.

They named their charming little daughter Vicki. Daddy John finally arrived on the scene shortly thereafter, delayed by weather and transportation problems. After a few days of recuperation, John, Roberta, and baby Vicki returned to Manila.

Meanwhile, Bill's condition improved sufficiently to allow a flight to Manila for a neurosurgical consultation. He needed special X-ray studies to enable us to determine what was causing the seizures.

A TIME TO WEEP, AGAIN

At that time we depended on the JAARS plane from Wycliffe base to help us out in emergency evacuations. Their base in Nasuli was located about 15 miles (24 kilometers) from Malaybalay. Not only are their pilots skillful, but they are all trained as expert aircraft mechanics. Bill and Marilyn were flown to Cagayan de Oro City, about 70 miles (112 kilometers) north, making connections with the commercial flight to Manila. Their children stayed at the Wycliffe base until Bill's medical problem could be settled.

The X-rays needed were studies of the arteries of the brain, since the working diagnosis was a stroke; however, a brain tumor produces similar symptoms. Back then, no million dollar machines provided computerized axial tonography (CAT) scans. In Bill's case, x-rays revealed a suspicious area in the right frontal lobe of the brain. The neurologist affirmed that such findings require surgery to make a conclusive diagnosis and to remove the problem.

Dr. Pardo, a neurosurgeon of good repute, accepted the case. The surgery would be done in Saint Luke's Hospital in Manila. Bill was admitted and the laboratory tests were done. We were asked to recruit donors for blood transfusions which would be needed during surgery. Here was the **rub**: Bill's type was B, with an Rh *negative* subtype!

That blood type is rare, especially in Orientals. To find even one donor in Manila, a city with over five million people at that time, would require a miracle. We notified prayer partners; we consulted the U.S. Embassy's medical department, and phoned Faith Academy and the U.S. military bases at Subic Bay and Sangley Point. A Navy chaplain took the responsibility of finding donors as a personal challenge. And he *found* them — four U.S. sailors. Navy helicopters flew them to Manila. They landed on the Embassy's heliopad in the middle of the night preceding the scheduled surgery. God supplied our need through these generous and compassionate strangers.

The surgery took about six hours. The brain lesion was not a cancer, but an area the size of a golf ball had lost its blood supply. This was indeed a type of stroke. Loved ones wept for joy. Bill should fully recover. The process was not without some complications, however, hiccups were a nuisance for about 11 days. Nevertheless, Bill slowly regained his strength and in due time was discharged from the hospital. The family was required to reside in Manila for six months before the neurologists were satisfied that Stevensons could leave for Malaybalay. The children returned to Faith Academy while Bill continued treatment in the city.

AND A TIME TO LAUGH, AGAIN
We were all delighted when the Stevensons returned home to Malaybalay. After a few months of recuperation, Bill resumed clinic work. Two years later the family left the Philippines for their regular furlough.

Upon their return, they were ready for a new assignment and went to the new mission hospital on the island of Leyte, about 150 miles (240 kilometers) to the northeast, in a town called Hilongos. Bill and Marilyn were especially well suited to that assignment and accepted the challenge with enthusiasm. Until their retirement in 1987, they made Leyte their base of operations. They teamed up with two younger ABWE couples: the Steve Holmans and the Jim Latzkos. Through the clinic ministry several Baptist churches were opened and eventually pastored by qualified Filipino brethren.

GOALS OF MEDICAL MISSIONS:
"And Jesus came and spake unto them, saying, All power is given

unto me in heaven and in earth. Go ye therefore, and *teach* all nations, *baptizing* them in the name of the Father, and of the Son, and of the Holy Ghost: *teaching* them to observe all things whatsoever I have commanded you: and lo, I am with you alway, even unto the end of the world" (Matthew 28:18-20).

1. **EVANGELISM**: *"making disciples"* must take top priority. In the mission hospitals this takes on various forms: pre-clinic gospel services led by the chaplain or missionary on duty; personal evangelism in the out-patient waiting rooms or at the bedside by both the chaplains and the hospital staff; and life-style evangelism, which means demonstrating Christian love as the hospital personnel care for the patient.

2. **LOCAL CHURCH AFFILIATION**: *"baptizing them"* implies that Biblical instruction is given to help the new believer follow the Lord. This includes teaching about water baptism as a public testimony. Since this is an ordinance of the local church, it constitutes the official introduction of the new believer into fellowship with a local body of believers. To aid the new convert in joining a group of believers, the mission clinics send his name and address to the pastor of the Baptist church nearest his home. In this way, the clinics help in the growth of the Bible-teaching churches throughout that area. In Bukidnon, for instance, there were 20 Baptist churches in the province when the clinic first opened. Today there are more than 200 local churches in the Bukidnon Association of Fundamental Baptist Churches (BAFBC)[1].

3. **DISCIPLING**: *"teaching them to observe all that I commanded you."* Obviously, not every convert in the mission hospitals can be tutored by the medical personnel. One of the most helpful programs in discipleship at Bethel Baptist Hospital was introduced by the medical director, the surgeon, and the pastor of the nearby Baptist church. Each month they held a three-day seminar to upgrade the provincial pastors and lay workers in discipling new believers. The results were almost explosive in developing an enthusiasm for following up new

[1] Appendix B

believers. Best of all, their churches grew appreciably. Quality care is also essential. It is true that often "actions speak louder than words." If you are the patient coming to a medical facility, you are doing so with the hope of finding the best care possible for your illness. Anything less is not acceptable, especially in a Christian clinic or hospital. Furthermore, the patient must know that he is accepted regardless of race, creed, or financial status. Excellence in care is certainly prescribed in God's Word: "Whatsoever ye do, do all to the glory of God" (I Corinthians 10:31), and, "Whatsoever thy hand findeth to do, do it with thy might" (Ecclesiastes 9:10).

The Stevenson family provides a good illustration of how these goals were implemented. Shortly after they moved to Hilongos, Leyte to help open the new mission hospital, Bill admitted a man named Leonardo Arinas. He came with his wife, Rose, from the other side of the island for medical care. After a prolonged period of treatment for tuberculosis, Leonardo's health greatly improved.

But more importantly, through daily attendance at the clinic gospel service, both he and his wife found new life in Christ. When he was clinically well enough to return home, he decided to remain in Hilongos until he could complete a basic course in Bible doctrine. He reasoned that when he did return home, he then would be able to teach his own relatives and friends those truths.

Leonardo eventually became the leader of a new church on the east coast of Leyte. Because of the spiritual awakening that resulted, the Stevensons felt they should transfer to the town of Abuyog. They set up a medical office as an auxiliary of the hospital. The ABWE team established on the eastern coast of Leyte two more Baptist churches, the largest in the capital city of Tacloban.

Where are Bill and Marilyn now? After 20 years of productive missionary life they retired. They moved back to New Jersey, and keep busy in their church and community. A "time to weep and a time to laugh" go on for the grandparents of 36 grandchildren and four great-grandchildren.

11
GONE TO THE DOGS

"To every thing there is a season, ...a time to kill,
and a time to heal" (Ecclesiastes 3:1,3).

Let me be transparent: I dislike dogs. I realize this jeopardizes friendship with dog-lovers, so I try to suppress my reactions. I'm on friendly terms with a few dogs. An intelligent, gentle golden retriever named Buffy and I get along well. German shepherds make good watchdogs but can be vicious. Drooling boxers turn my stomach. Miniature breeds like terriers and poodles make me wonder if they are toys with batteries: cute but vain. Some dogs seem to take on the temperaments of their masters, which may or may not be complimentary.

But I have several reasons for my antipathy. The majority of free-running dogs in countries where we have worked are mongrels. Those mange-afflicted flea-bags run in packs, fighting with one another interminably. I've been surrounded by such packs, howling and snapping at my heels. When that happens during an emergency call to the hospital at three o'clock in the morning, I fail to find warmth in my heart for those creatures. The noise of their howling and snarling and barking has kept us awake too often.

However, the major reason for my distemper over dogs is that I have seen the horror caused by rabies, known as *hydrophobia*. A major symptom of this malady is fear of drinking water because the swallowing muscles are paralyzed and water chokes the victim.

Rabies is a disease caused by a virus carried in the saliva of an infected animal. Once a patient develops the symptoms, it is incurable. The usual carrier of the disease in developing countries is a rabid dog. Other potential carriers include bats, raccoons, jackals, squirrels, skunks, and -- rarely -- cats. The rabid dog is recognized by its erratic behavior, weakness in the hind-quarters, frothing at the mouth, and inability to swallow.

One such mutt staggered into the hospital compound while we were busy in the clinic. Before long our ten-year-old-son Dave ran to us with the marks of the dog's bite on his leg. Within a very few minutes, a worker carried in our younger son Mike in similar condition. Both had been bitten by the dog as he careened across the yard where the children were playing. We frantically began scrubbing the wounds and administering the anti-rabies injections.

The anti-rabies vaccine available in the late 1950's and 1960's was prepared from the serum of horses which had been immunized with the rabies virus. The injections were given under the skin of the abdomen once daily for three weeks. The boys were good about coming to the clinic for their shots during the ten o'clock morning break. Each time their bravery was rewarded with a cookie and a soft drink. Since the series of injections causes tender areas of inflammation at each site, these can be quite uncomfortable. The boys eagerly looked forward to the last of the injections. So the 21st injection was cause for a major celebration.

But the next day, Mike (then age four) showed up at the usual ten o'clock appointment time. We were all surprised that he forgot he had completed the series. His response was, "Oh, I just came for my cookie." Smart kid! The boys did not get rabies.

The immunizations do not always prevent the disease. A baby boy I had delivered at Bethel Hospital was not as fortunate. His missionary parents lived in a town about 62 miles (100 kilometers) away. While the child was still a toddler playing on the kitchen floor of their home, a rabid dog dashed into the house, bit the child on the face and fled. The panic-stricken parents rushed the child to the nearest doctor who immediately began the series of injections. The virus, however, quickly established the infection. Since the wound was so much closer to the brain, within a very few days the child died. You can imagine the grief that followed.

Subsequently, the mission council decided that every sick dog that appeared on the compound must be killed. The ABWE mission hospital in Bangladesh has a policy of destroying all stray dogs and jackals that wander onto their property. Pet dogs and cats must be immunized against rabies. Fortunately, today the rabies vaccine for humans is much safer and more effective and is made from human serum globulin.

I don't particularly like dogs. But that didn't deter fellow missionaries from having such pets. And I must admit that some of those canines were cute, friendly and even necessary for security. Robberies are commonplace. Probably most expatriates in the Philippines have a watchdog or two, often a German shepherd or Doberman pinscher — the fiercer, the better.

We did have a pet monkey for a few months. We kept him tethered to a tree out in the side yard. A tribal patient gave the monkey to me as payment for his clinic fee. During the earlier years of the clinic, patients coming from distant villages in the mountains often brought produce or livestock to pay for medicines. We were paid with chickens more than once. Of course, it isn't too difficult to convert the fowl into an edible dish, but monkeys?

The kids wanted us to keep the primate. It was just a little thing and had a winsome expression on its face. We kept it, and the kids named him Moomoy. For some unknown reason, the monkey took a liking to me and to Aunt Millie. He squealed at us whenever we were within range. His special interest was sitting on my shoulder and checking through my hair. For some reason, he never caught on to the fact that I did *not* harbor lice, which he considered a delicacy. He checked anyway.

However, he was not too friendly with the children from off the compound who teased him unmercifully. Consequently, as he grew up he became more and more hostile to kids and would bite in self-defense.

Another problem was that he sometimes slipped out of his pelvic harness, a hazard on more than one occasion. Our neighbor's dogs disliked monkeys. As long as the monkey stayed in his tree, the dogs couldn't get at him. But during his dashes for freedom, he was free game for the dogs. Once we were certain his days were over. One of the dogs had caught him and taken his head into his mouth and shaken him into unconsciousness. The kids rescued him in time and brought him to the clinic. Moomoy survived that attack.

Once he got loose while we were in church. The congregation was celebrating the monthly communion service. I sometimes officiated at those services when the pastor was away. I was up front leading the congregation in the opening hymn when I saw, to my horror, Moomoy proudly prancing along the back of the rear pew. I feared he might see me at the communion table and race down to join in the proceedings.

To my great relief, Millie was sitting in one of the back pews and she saw him first. With a minimum of disturbance, she drew within striking distance and grabbed the monkey. The sigh of relief which escaped my lips must have been considered an unspoken prayer. No one seemed to notice. Not many days thereafter, we sent Moomoy back to life in the jungle.

Probably if we had had a dog we might have prevented a couple of house robberies. Lenore was alone in the house in Leyte while I was away for a few days. In the wee hours of the morning she was awakened by what she thought were scratching sounds. *Probably rats again*, she thought. But in her drowsy state she lay quietly. Then the thin light of a penlight caught her attention in the bedroom across the hall, and she knew she was not alone.

Stifling panic Lenore reached for the dinner bell which she had thoughtfully placed on the floor next to the head of her bed. Breathing a prayer *Lord, help me yell*, she grasped the bell and rang it with all her might while screaming, "NOSOR!"

Nosor was the nickname of the hospital accountant who had quarters downstairs. His full name was Nebuchadnezzar Cacho. He immediately recognized an emergency in Lenore's call and yelled a reply as he dashed out of his room and ran up the back stairs. Before long neighborhood dogs were barking, hospital personnel were running and the whole compound was in a stir. Such was the power of my wife's alarm.

By the time Nosor arrived, however, the invaders had disappeared, leaving behind the miscellaneous treasures they had planned to carry off with them. The thief had cut an opening in the front porch screen. He had then removed a couple louvers of the window and made his entrance. But that had been done so quietly, Lenore was not disturbed. The intruder had even snacked on a banana and an egg from the refrigerator to sate his appetite. What had awakened Lenore was the sound of his opening letters on our desk in his search for cash. Lenore was in the adjacent bedroom, which would have been his next stop had she not yelled.

When Lenore checked for missing items, she found the tape recorder had been taken and a few items were bundled near the door awaiting the thief's exit. From then on, some of the girls from the hospital volunteered to stay with her nights until I returned. How thankful we all were that Lenore had not been molested!

Of course, if you own pets, you must take care of them. Missionary doctors are often asked by owners for help with sick animals. Most of the time, I referred them to the government veterinarian if he was in town. His usual recommendation for a sick or wounded animal was to put it out of its misery. But that is not always acceptable to a caring owner. I even found that I benefitted from an experience of operating on a dog.

The dog was a much-loved pet Doberman pinscher. A car accident had broken the dog's hind leg. The vet didn't do surgery and advised the animal be put down, but its owner's children wouldn't allow that. So the dog was brought to our doorstep. I couldn't resist the plea and decided to take an x-ray to verify the degree of injury. The film showed a clean, spiral break in the femur that would not heal properly without an operation.

Public relations are vitally important to us expatriates. "Love me, love my dog" is not an idle comment in some circumstances. A decision was in the balance. We had the wherewithal to do something about this problem, and the next day *was* an "off day" — the clinic would be closed. The scale weighed in favor of doing the surgery. I would benefit by gaining orthopedic experience in the process.

A medical student from America on a three-month visit to learn about mission medical work was on hand and eager to assist. He prepared the canine patient, eagerly helped by our daughter Shirley who was on a semester break from high school. She was fond of dogs and this dog seemed fond of her. An intravenous anesthesia, ketamine, was given the dog. We observed sterile surgical technique. The incision was made over the break and the femoral fracture carefully aligned. Stainless steel bone screws secured the proper fixation. The wound was closed and the leg put in a splint, then the owners took the dog home for tender loving care.

The last we heard, the dog was running as agilely as ever. And Bethel Clinic had an A-1 rating on the PR scale. As a seal of approval, the Lord brought a Christian veterinarian to Bethel when the surgical consultant married Dr. Blessie. Now Malaybalay has a caring, licensed doctor of animals whose witness for the Lord among the more affluent pet-owners in the area is bearing eternal dividends.

This topic about animal care adds interest and significance to the reading of such passages in scripture as in Matthew 10:29-32:

> Are not two sparrows sold for a farthing? And one of them shall not fall on the ground without your Father. But the very hairs of your head are all numbered. Fear ye not therefore, ye are of more value than many sparrows. Whosoever therefore shall confess me before men, him will I confess also before my Father which is in heaven.

When a patient comes into the clinic and I can find nothing physical to account for his symptoms, I ask about the pressures and anxieties in his life. Not infrequently he is blaming himself for something he should have done and didn't, or about something he did that he shouldn't have done: the "*if only*" thoughts. On the other hand, he may be worrying himself sick about the future and its uncertainties: the "*what if*" ideas.

If that patient is a professing believer in Christ, I get out my prescription pad and write the remedy. Rx: Memorize Philippians 4:6-7 and quote it as needed:

> Be anxious for nothing; but in everything by prayer and supplication with thanksgiving let your requests be made known unto God. And the peace of God, which passeth all understanding, shall keep your hearts and your minds through Christ Jesus.

If God is interested in the downfall of one of the least of His creations, how much greater concern has He for mankind?

12
KEPT!

"The LORD shall preserve thee from all evil:
he shall preserve thy soul.
The LORD shall preserve thy going out and thy coming in
from this time forth, and even for evermore"
(Psalm 121:7,8).

"Didn't you ever get sick? After all, you had to deal with all kinds of illnesses. Some were probably very contagious. Weren't you always living in fear?" friends inquire.

Not really. Our five children had the usual childhood diseases as they were growing up. And Lenore and I suffered the occasional inconvenience of common colds and the like. But working in a foreign country was not more dangerous for us than living in America. Considering the pace of life in the USA and its expanding plague of incurable viruses, I believe we had fewer risks in the Philippines.

Some people have the idea that a missionary is a preacher wearing khaki shirt and shorts and a pith helmet, trekking jungle trails with a Bible in one hand and a rifle in the other. For instance, we received a letter asking, "Do you live in a cottage or just an 'imaginary' grass hut?" Perhaps our reply was a shock: we dress in casual summer clothing; live in comfortable quarters; and drive to town in a car when necessary.

For us, going to work each morning meant crossing an expanse of lawn between our house and the clinic. We didn't have to fight rush-hour traffic on congested highways. During our first few years in the town of Malaybalay we would joke that the local definition of "heavy traffic" meant two vehicles passing within the same hour. Consequently, the hospital didn't receive many victims of traffic accidents. However, a few years later, the situation changed: the main highway was asphalted; then came an increase in casualties. All of our missionary career, we lived in provincial settings. Quality medical care by well trained physicians was not in short supply in the *cities* of the Philippines. About 4000 medical students graduate each year from 27 medical colleges in that country. Although half of these graduates seek overseas medical residency programs to further their education, the others set up practices in their homeland. However, those whose goal is financial gain will go where the affluent live: the cities.

For this reason, many people living in the provinces seldom see a physician. Indeed, some go an entire lifetime without consulting a doctor. Instead, they rely on the "barefoot doctors" who are untrained and use herbs, massage, and folk-medicines. Tribal people living in interior villages consult healers who deal in spirit worship and practice animal sacrifice to appease the angry spirits. Life expectancy figures attest to their plight. If a citizen reaches his 60's, he's considered fortunate, and *old!*

One of the policies of the medical department of ABWE in the Philippines is that our medical facilities are to be based in provincial areas where medical help is not readily available. That has invariably required a compound set-up. The hospital compound has living quarters for personnel on the same grounds, usually, with a residence for single women and apartments for married personnel. ABWE supporters contribute to the cost of building those facilities, but the upkeep and current expenses are the responsibility of the medical unit itself, and the personnel occupying the quarters.

In thinking over the opening question in this chapter, we do recall a few narrow escapes. I'm sure that from God's perspective those were designed to strengthen our faith as we experienced incidents in which His angels performing their duties. Probably we were protected from countless other near-tragedies that we didn't even know about.

For He shall give His angels charge over thee, to keep thee
in all thy ways. They shall bear thee up in their hands, lest
thou dash thy foot against a stone (Psalm 91:11-12).

One of those incidents occurred on the highway which ran
northward through our town to the coast. The missionaries involved
primarily were the Wilhites,[1] who had recently arrived to begin their
first term. Mabel was pregnant at the time and within a few weeks
she delivered a lovely baby boy at Bethel Baptist Clinic.

About a month after the delivery when Mabel had fully recovered,
the Wilhites were ready for an excursion. They decided to drive to
the northern city of Cagayan de Oro, about 70 miles (112 kilometers)
away, to do some shopping. Orlan was eager to exercise the new
Jeep station wagon they had brought with them from Toledo, Ohio.

They invited Priscilla, Davie and Lenore to join them. I did not
go along; I had work to do at the clinic. Besides, the idea of a bumpy
four-hour ride to the coast, followed by walking around in a hot city
just didn't appeal to me. So I waved them good-bye and figured on
seeing them in about 10 hours.

But within three hours a truck came roaring into the yard. In the
front seat were three palefaced missionaries: the two Wilhites and
Priscilla. Mabel had a bloody rag wound about her head. Lenore
was not in sight, nor was our neighbor Davie.

"Lenore is all right!" shouted Priscilla as she jumped from the
truck. That was a comfort, to say the least. But it was obvious that
Mabel and Orlan Wilhite were not in great condition. While Ron
questioned the truck driver, Priscilla and I helped Mabel into the
minor operating room. Our examination revealed a three-inch
laceration across Mabel's forehead at the hairline. After cleaning
and suturing the wound, I applied a sterile dressing and took her to a
bed on the ward. Orlan was in an adjacent bed with cracked ribs and
a painful chest.

Then we learned what had happened. After the group left the
hospital, the Jeep hummed along the winding road with everyone
cheerily conversing. But as they neared the floor of one of the three
canyons, the road narrowed. Unexpectedly, around the next bend

[1] Appendix A

came a red flat-bed cargo truck occupying most of the road. Orlan tried to swerve out of the path of the oncoming truck, bringing the Jeep perilously close to the edge of the road.

The projecting body of the truck struck the Jeep just behind the driver's seat, knocking it backwards over the cliff. The first ten or twelve feet were a shear drop, followed by a less abrupt descent to the raging river below. The station wagon jolted down in an upright position, rear-end first, intermittently slowed by vegetation.

"We're *gawnuz!*" yelled Priscilla as they careened through the underbrush toward the river, her Boston accent strongly evident. Lenore, in the middle of the back seat, watched out the rear window, praying that *something* would stop the fall.

About 80 feet down the car came to an abrupt halt. The rear wheels were in the river, a big rock stopping further descent. A quick inventory revealed that only Mabel in the front seat had much of a problem: the bleeding wound on her forehead. They wrapped her head with a t–shirt dipped into the cold mountain water that lapped at the Jeep's door. The missionaries then slowly and laboriously started to climb back up the embankment.

Workmen on the highway thought they were seeing ghosts! How could anyone have survived that fall? But the men finally came to their senses enough to help them up. By then the offending truck had pulled to the shoulder of the road, to imply that it had always been on the correct side of the highway. And there he planned to stay until the "evidence" was documented by a traffic officer.

Of course, back then, people in the next passing vehicle could take a message to the nearest constabulary command post. If anyone was available, they *might* come to check. Meanwhile, Mabel needed medical care.

Seeing the blood-soaked improvised bandage wrapped on Mabel's forehead, and being bombarded by the authoritative persuasion of the *Americanos*, the truck driver finally got the message. The injured couple and Priscilla were loaded onto the seat next to the driver and they roared off. Lenore and Davie waited on the highway for the next vehicle that would pass their way to take them back to

Malaybalay. They waited 45 minutes.

You can imagine that there was great rejoicing at the goodness of the Lord in preserving their lives that day. God wasn't finished with them yet! It was a different story for the Jeep; a crane was required to get the wreck out of the river and up the embankment. The insurance company declared the station wagon totaled.

Orlan and Mabel were in hospital beds. Orlan was bemoaning the loss of the station wagon but grateful to be alive. Mabel was back in the same hospital bed she had vacated only a few weeks before. Undoubtedly her mind wandered back to the details of *that* admission. When she was certain she was in labor, she had sent Orlan to inform us. The nervous father appeared at our door to announce that Mabel was in need of our attention.

After checking her, I agreed that she should be admitted to the ward. In those earlier days, we admitted patients requiring surgical or obstetrical care to quarters on the ground floor of our residence. We had a two-bed ward, and a multi-purpose room for technical procedures.

The nurses prepared for the upcoming event. This gave me time to advise Paul Friedrichsen of the imminent birth. Paul was one of ABWE's pioneer church-planting evangelists, visiting our area on a special assignment to film various aspects of the ABWE work. We thought it would be interesting to have a film segment showing the medical missionaries busy at work, delivering the baby of another ABWE family.

Paul had talked this over with the Wilhites, who gave their permission. All Paul had to do was to discreetly set up the 16 mm movie camera, microphones, and lights so as to have a film that could be shown in churches and mission societies back in America.

Now the time had come! Paul positioned himself and his camera in a closet which opened at the head of the delivery table. A second door in that closet opened into the carport at the rear, giving him easy, unobstructed access. He placed the microphone where it would catch the joyous sounds of the baby's first cry. Unfortunately, that closet was about the size of a phone booth, and quite warm. But Paul was satisfied. The program must go on. The camera whirred; the baby boy cried on cue; and apparently all was recorded for posterity. We noted that Paul didn't show up for supper that evening. Upon inquiry we learned that he wasn't feeling too well. After all, it was *his* first delivery.

Paul left for another leg of his appointed rounds and we didn't see him for several months. But when we did see him, our first question was, "How did the film of the Wilhite delivery turn out?"

"You're not going to believe this," said he. "I forgot to put film in the camera." So much for his motion picture career.

The loss of the film, followed by the loss of the Jeep, all faded into insignificance as Orlan and Mabel praised God for their survival to raise their lovely family and to serve their gracious Lord.

Missionaries have to come to grips with priorities. Someone has well said, "Be sure you control your possessions rather than your possessions controlling you!" Over the years we have lost material things to fire, floods, typhoons, thefts, breakage, and accidents. Vastly more important are relationships. Number one is our relationship to God. The apostle Paul brought this into focus when he wrote:

> For I am persuaded, that neither death, nor life, nor angels, nor principalities, nor powers, nor things present, nor things to come, nor height, nor depth, nor any other creature, shall be able to separate us from the love of God, which is in Christ Jesus our Lord (Romans 8:38-39).

How practical, then, are the word of Christ in His Sermon on the Mount:

> Therefore take no thought, saying, What shall we eat? Or, What shall we drink? Or, Wherewithal shall we be clothed? (For after all these things do the Gentiles seek:) for your heavenly Father knoweth that ye have need of all these things. But seek ye first the kingdom of God, and His righteousness; and all these things shall be added unto you. Take therefore no thought for the morrow: for tomorrow shall take thought for the things of itself. Sufficient unto the day is the evil thereof (Matthew 6:31-34).

13

ON EAGLES' WINGS

"They that wait upon the Lord shall renew their strength;
they shall mount up with wings as eagles;
they shall run, and not be weary; they shall walk, and not faint"
(Isaiah 40:31).

I appreciated those reassuring words in Isaiah when I was returning from Manila after attending a meeting. Although we usually had to fly on the commercial airline, whenever possible I would try to hitch a ride on a mission plane if one were available. Happily, on this return flight to Mindanao, I was invited to ride in Vern Anderson's Cherokee-Six. He had his plane in Manila and was due to leave the day I was to fly home.

Vern was the senior missionary with another mission. His base of operation was on the north coast of Mindanao, west of Cagayan de Oro City about 50 miles (66 kilometers). He was convinced of the need for private plane service for their personnel because their location was remote from adequate medical help in an emergency.

For example, his own daughter suffered from a ruptured appendix prior to their having a plane. She nearly died while he tried to find a doctor who could operate. That convinced Vern that something had to be done. His temperament was such that he decided to become a pilot himself. He took flying lessons in a rented plane, and concentrated so intensely on mastering the skills required for licensure that within about a week he was ready to solo. He passed the flight tests and obtained his license. Supporters in America donated funds for a plane. Vern became a frequent flyer, often landing on the grass landing strip on the edge of Malaybalay, bringing patients for urgent care.

Vern had been the catalyst for my taking up flying. He knew I had recently returned from furlough with a pilot's license, so he told me to take the left seat and fly us home. Also in the plane were three other missionary men heading for Mindanao, including Bob Griffin, the chief pilot of JAARS. Bob took the co-pilot's seat while Vern sat behind us with the others.

We took off. The exhilaration of heading home and flying the plane made the day extra special. I leveled off at 5,500 feet and trimmed the plane for the cruise. Visibility was unlimited. The beauty of those 7,000 emerald islands which comprise the Philippines can be appreciated best from the air.

After leaving the coastline of Luzon and cruising over the island of Mindoro we came to the open Philippine Sea. We checked the gauges registering the fuel level in all four tanks, two in each wing. Bob switched us off the left main tank to the right, and we flew on for several minutes. However, in watching the gauges, we noted that the gasoline was still being drained from the left main tank only. So he switched to the right tip tank. In a few minutes we knew that we were still on the left main tank. The tumbler switch was apparently not working.

"Link, head for the nearest island with a sufficiently long sandy beach while I try to fix this switch," Bob remarked.

I could see only one island within range off our left wing-tip, but the beach appeared to be long enough. I turned toward that island. Bob squirmed around to work under the second seat where the switches were located. The problem was that the seat was occupied by a couple of men who had to assume a standing crouch position to lift the cover. But no matter how they tried, it became obvious that the switch could not be fixed while we were in the air.

We had about five minutes of fuel remaining in the left main tank. Our only hope was to make an emergency beach landing if the gas tank didn't empty first. The open sea beneath us didn't look inviting with its shark infested waters.

"MAYDAY! MAYDAY!" The transmitter carried our radio message to the JAARS base in Mindanao.

We were all grateful to have aboard a seasoned pilot who had logged thousands of flight hours. Bob and I switched seats for the landing as we approached the one island within reach of our dwindling fuel supply.

Bob radioed the coordinates of our location. We were about to make an emergency landing on an island called Burias, to the northeast of Masbate island. The operator got the message and was alerted to stand by.

Bob figured that we had just enough fuel for one pass over the island. What we thought was one long beach turned out to be two, with a tongue of rocks forming a short peninsula between them. People crowded the northern beach — the whole town seemed to be there. The southern beach was empty and long enough for a landing. As we observed this from an altitude of about 700 feet, Bob set up his turns and we came in for the landing. One attempt was all we had. The fuel tank was reading empty.

Bob's expertise paid off. The landing was smooth on packed sand just above the water line. The engine sputtered and stopped. We all piled out, praising the Lord! We made radio contact to advise the base of the safe landing and to schedule a time to stand by for a progress report.

Now we had another problem: the tide was coming in. The plane had to be moved to higher ground immediately. By this time, all those people who had been on the northern beach swarmed the plane. One of the men explained that they had gathered to celebrate John the Baptist Day. That Catholic holiday called for water sports. When we flew in, the celebrants thought a politician had arrived to make a speech.

We corrected that misconception and told them that the *plane* was in imminent danger of being "baptized." Almost before we knew it, men were under each of the low-slung wings of the Cherokee. At the command of a leader they straightened up in unison and marched up the incline. "Where shall we put it, sir?" They were quite used to that sort of work. They still move their small country houses in a similar way: manpower.

Problem two was the faulty switch, but Bob made short work of that. After the back seat was emptied and removed, he had access to the switch box. Within a few minutes the tumbler was corrected.

Problem three was the length of the beach. Compared to the length of field needed for landing, a much longer runway is needed for take-off. The pilots measured it off: too short, unless the tide was out and the plane was not encumbered with extra weight.

We all got busy. The plane's contents were stripped out. Only the pilot's seat was left in place. Vern, who owned the Cherokee, wanted to take the full responsibility of getting his pride and joy off that beach when the tide was out. The fishermen on the island knew the time of low-tide: five o'clock in the afternoon, about six hours hence.

We hired two out-rigger motor boats for the trip to Masbate and loaded all the cargo into them. We had time to explain to the islanders why we had to land on their shores. They considered us "lucky." We countered with the assurance we had that God was in charge of the trip and of our lives; we were in His capable hands. Furthermore, perhaps He had brought us to their island for a purpose: to bring them the Good News that they were loved by this almighty heavenly Father.

The boat trip was slow and noisy, and the sun was merciless. The crossing took about eight hours. As we traveled, we each had time to meditate and enjoy the beauty of the sunset. Then the curtain of darkness fell as we sailed into the harbor of Masbate City. We unloaded and went immediately to the house of missionary friends living there: the Dick Varberg family. He was renowned for being "Mr. Fix-it" and we could use some fixing. At that time we didn't realize how major the fixing project would be.

We assumed that Vern and the plane would be there by that time, though we had neither seen nor heard it during our voyage. For one thing, in the tropics sunset regularly occurs between 6:00 and 6:30 in the afternoon whether it is winter or summer. Perhaps he had flown

The Nelson quartet: Dave and Becky join Lenore and Link at a church service.

Patients began to come from miles around for surgical procedures.

Link is inducted as a Fellow of the Philippine College of Surgeons in 1973.

Lenore spent part of her day in the pharmacy of Bethel Baptist Hospital, Malaybalay.

18th Annual Conference of Bukidnon Association of Baptist Churches.

We're off on a trek through the mountains of Bukidnon to attend a Short-Term Bible Institute.

Link and the Aunties participate in a tent meeting during an evangelistic campaign in Linabo; young David Nelson joins in, too.

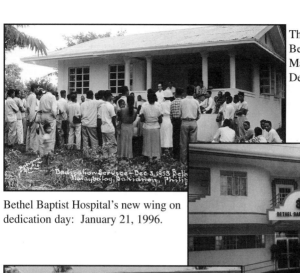

The dedication service for Bethel Baptist Hospital, Malaybalay, Bukidnon -- December 3, 1953.

Bethel Baptist Hospital's new wing on dedication day: January 21, 1996.

Leyte Baptist Clinic & Hospital staff with ABWE missionaries.

Palawan Baptist Hospital, Roxas, Palawan.

Aklan Baptist Hospital opened its doors in 1982.

The Cessna-180 was the ABWE work-horse for getting us around. Not all of the airstrips were first class.

Sometimes the plane lands in the more remote villages of Palawan.

over after dark and we hadn't noticed. But no, he wasn't at the airstrip. About midnight, after we had all found a place to lie down in the Varberg house, someone called at the door: Vern. He had attempted to take off the beach with the tide out, but a wave had rolled in just at the end of his take-off run. The wave caught the seaward wheel and pulled the plane into the sea. The islanders carried the plane back up the beach, but the water ruined the engine. A major overhaul was required.

After a short nap, Dick rounded up a crew of men plus lumber and tools, and roared off in a couple of motorized *bancas* (out-rigger boats) to the island of Burias. Bob, the pilot-mechanic, and Vern, the owner of the plane, went along. They worked long and hard for two days, disassembling the plane and floating it back for repairs in a hangar at the airport on Masbate.

The rest of us headed for our homes and work, flying on a Philippine Airlines DC3 which made a scheduled stop on Masbate only two days a week. Our wives welcomed us back. They had been advised by the JAARS radio operator that we were all safe and sound, so they were not to worry.

But let me give you a sequel to the story. The Baptist churches on the island of Masbate followed up this airplane incident by keeping in touch with the citizens on Burias. Now 13 Baptist churches stand on that island as a direct result of our dropping in unexpectedly for a few hours.

Many missions have an aviation department. Outstanding among them is the JAARS division of Wycliffe Bible Translators. From our experience in the Philippines, we know that lives have been saved because of those skillful men and their equipment. Mission Aviation Fellowship (MAF) is another such organization, founded on the precept that pilots and planes are essential for missionary work in the more remote parts of the world where commercial aviation is not available. We were grateful for the JAARS and MAF pilots and planes ready to help us in emergencies on several occasions while they were in the Philippines. Shirley Abbott, a Wycliffe Bible Translator, will attest to that.

Shirley's base was across a mountain range from Bethel Baptist Hospital in Malaybalay. To hike into that area would take several days. As in many such remote locations, JAARS had laid out the plans and implemented the construction of a landing field sufficiently long to accommodate their work-horse planes, the Helio Couriers. Those STOL (Short Take-Off and Landing) aircraft can maneuver into and depart from very short runways at relatively slow speeds. Shirley was only about 25 minutes by air from the mission hospital. Her base had short-wave radio contact with both the JAARS hangar and my office.

My schedule was to stand by for medical emergency calls around six o'clock every morning, and again around four in the afternoon when the translators had their network open for calls from tribal locations. It was one of those afternoons when Shirley called me and began describing the symptoms of one of her patients: nausea, vomiting, low-grade fever and increasingly painful lower abdomen. Upon further questioning, I was convinced she was describing an atttack of acute appendicitis.

"Who is the patient, Shirley?" I asked, expecting her to name one of the tribal people. After a longer pause than necessary, she answered, "I am."

Bob Griffin was on the JAARS end of the net by this time and knew Shirley needed an air evacuation as soon as possible. "Shirley, what's the weather like there?" Unfortunately, it was socked in with a late afternoon fog and mist. All Bob could do was await better weather.

Clear skies greeted Bob at dawn, but Shirley's voice had a quiver in it as she related the news: "It's fogged in here right down to the ground." You can be sure praying colleagues were busy interceding for Shirley and the weather. A few hours later, she reported a slight break in the clouds over her area and Bob took off. He crossed the mountain and flew over the valley where her tiny village was located. He searched the clouds for a hole through which he could descend, and finally found one.

Upon landing, he found Shirley doubled in pain. She had to be carried to the plane and strapped into the rear seat. At full throttle, Bob took off, poked a hole in the clouds and soared into glorious sunshine. Only 20 minutes later Shirley was being taken from the plane at the hospital air-strip.

The surgery seemed almost anticlimactic when compared with the evacuation flight. All went smoothly. The inflamed appendix was removed without complications. Another few hours' delay could have been disastrous. But God had His plans for Shirley and her partner, Pat Hartung, to complete work on the Bible translation for that tribe tucked away in the valley on the far side of the mountain.

Missionaries must remember that they are expendable as they serve the Lord. His ways are not necessarily our ways. One morning during Christmas week 1968, Lenore and I tuned in our short-wave radio to the frequency of the Far Eastern Broadcasting Company (FEBC), a Christian station out of Manila. That was our breakfast-time custom which kept us more current on world affairs. But on this particular morning a news-flash interrupted the program. The announcer stated that a missionary plane had crashed in Palawan. The report mentioned fatalities. They were awaiting the details of the tragedy.

Immediately we came alert. We knew that two missions had planes on that island, and our ABWE colleagues often flew with them. I rushed next door to our neighbor, Clif Carlburg, who was the MAF pilot based in Malaybalay at the time. He caught the alarm in my voice as I broke the news. His hand shook as he tuned his short-wave transmitter radio to the MAF frequency in Palawan. One of their planes had crashed during a flight to carry supplies to a remote mission station. The pilot, George Raney, and his passenger, Merle Buckingham, were both killed.

Merle and his wife Joyce were ABWE missionaries. They had three children. Merle was a Bible teacher and a talented pianist. George was a skillful pilot with whom we had flown on previous medical trips to Palawan. His wife Beth had been monitoring his flight on the radio when the plane went down in a coconut grove. She was left to raise their three children and the baby in her womb.

Clif immediately flew to Palawan to assist the MAF and ABWE families and to support the bereaved through that difficult Christmas. We were all grief stricken. Though we would never learn the cause of the accident, none of us could doubt that our omniscient God had his purpose in such a seeming tragedy.

About ten years after that incident, when MAF moved their facilities to Indonesia in the early 1970's, ABWE was able to purchase one of their planes to begin our own aviation department. While we waited for pilots who were applying for appointment, Lowell Edwards, a World War II multi-engine pilot volunteered to get the Mindanao project off the ground. The mission required that he pass a rigid "bush-pilot" training course with MAF in California to qualify; that he did.

Upon his arrival in the Philippines, another MAF pilot checked him out on the Mindanao circuit. Before long Lowell and his wife Virginia became an essential part of the hospital team. Though retired, Lowell didn't lack energy or efficiency.

Our son Dave eventually became one of the ABWE pilots. When a teenager, Dave decided that he wanted to be a pilot. After graduating from Cedarville College, he earned his wings and his license as an aviation mechanic at the Moody School of Aviation in Elizabethton, Tennessee. He and his wife Becky, with their two boys, Jeff and Josh, joined us in Malaybalay in 1977. From then on, he flew us on our medical-mission trips. I confess to feeling a touch of pride whenever we flew with our son at the controls.

As other missionary pilots became available, a second plane was added to ABWE's Philippine fleet. That plane was based on the island of Palawan near the mission hospital which opened there in the latter half of the 1970's. Larry Holman and Harry Rogers were the skilled pilotmechanics that kept it flying for several years.

The ABWE aviation program closed in the Philippines toward the end of the 1980's. The reasons for that decision included the *cost* of flying and maintaining a private plane. It became cheaper to use commercial aviation which was reaching more areas of the country. Then, too, the mission medical facilities were becoming autonomous

WITH SCALPEL AND THE SWORD

as capable Filipino professionals took the place of the missionaries. JAARS and New Tribes Mission pilots were still available to air-lift medical emergencies.

Interestingly enough, we were on hand when another ABWE aviation program began in West Africa in 1994. Missionary pilot Randy Alderman uncrated the Cessna-205 at the mission hospital in Togo. It had been shipped across the Atlantic in a 40-foot container. The director of ABWE aviation, Hank Scheltema, arrived from the USA shortly thereafter and assisted in assembling the aircraft.

The next major project was preparing a safe landing field behind the mission hospital on the edge of the village of Tsiko, town of Kpele Adeta. Randy supervised clearing a strip nearly a mile (one kilometer) long and 33 yards (30 meters) wide through elephant grass. That was followed by grading and preparing a smooth, hard surface. It took nearly two years to finish. Now Randy is flying mercy flights and transporting missionaries in Togo.

The first patient to be airlifted was veteran missionary Kay Washer, who had come with her husband Dallas to Togo in 1974. The Washers were effective in evangelism and establishing churches. However, Dal and Kay were burdened with the number of blind people in that country and wanted to do something about their plight.

Through official channels in the Department of Health, they obtained permission to develop a center for the blind in Kpalime, a town about 93 miles (150 kilometers) north of Lome, the capital city. The children admitted to the center received a basic education. Furthermore, instruction in crafts developed confidence, earning ability, and a sense of self-worth in otherwise hopeless waifs.

Dal was also instrumental in planning for an ABWE hospital in Togo. Dr. David Clutts and I joined Dal in 1977 to survey a suitable site for the facility. With the advice and consent of the regional Togolese health officer, and with the guidance of the Lord, we found just what we were looking for near the town of Kpele Adeta, 19 miles (30 kilometers) from the blind center. Construction began and the hospital opened for patients in 1984. It was dedicated the *Karolyn Kempton Memorial Christian Hospital* in memory of the wife of

ABWE president, Wendell Kempton. Mrs. Kempton had died of a brain hemorrhage on December 12, 1980.

Another tragedy struck. Dal Washer had a massive heart attack while visiting this ABWE hospital in 1989 and died suddenly in spite of the heroic efforts of the hospital staff. Working with a competent staff of Togolese, Kay continued to pour her love into the blind center. But in the spring of 1996, Kay fell from a concrete step and severely fractured her leg. Her ABWE colleagues drove her to the mission hospital. The break was so complicated that the mission doctor placed her leg in a plaster cast and advised air-evacuation to the USA.

The landing field was ready for use. Randy revved up the mission plane and flew her and her nurse-companion to the commercial air terminal 125 miles (200 kilometers) away. This first air-evac event seemed to be the stamp of God's approval on that newly opened mission aviation department.

14
SOME THROUGH THE FIRE

"Some through the water, some through the flood,
Some through the fire, but all through the blood;
Some through great sorrow, but God gives a song;
In the night season and all the day long."
(G. A. Young)

We well remember the day that Bethel Baptist Clinic's infirmary building opened for business on August 8, 1955. The new addition was annexed to the outpatient clinic building, which had been completed two years earlier and remained the hub of daily medical activity. Attractive in their fresh coat of white paint, the cement-block buildings were functionally designed and roofed with corrugated, galvanized iron sheets. At last we had a place for nine in-patient hospital beds.

Previously, we had temporary accommodations for surgical and maternity patients in two rooms on the ground floor of our residence, a far from an ideal arrangement. We were eager to move these quarters to the new infirmary as soon as that was built.

The first admission to the infirmary was an emotion-packed event. Around 9:30 in the evening, I was working on correspondence in my office at home after the children were in bed for the night. The window facing me overlooked the mission house next door where Kaye Mollohan, Rosemary Ullery, and Alma Shoemaker[1] lived. Lenore was enjoying a get-together there with the women on the compound.

---

[1] Appendix A

Through the open windows I could hear them playing games, chattering, and laughing. Two guests of honor from the Wycliffe base were being entertained: Jan Forster and Myra Lou Barnard.

Then I heard the screams. Someone was frantically calling, "Link! Link!"

Racing down the front stairs, I saw that the kitchen of the women's house was ablaze. Even more frightening was the sight of Lenore running down the back stairs of that house with her clothes on fire! Cross-country running and jumping hurdles were not my strong events in college track, but that night my adrenalin was pumping. I leaped over a group of drums that stood in my way, raced to my wife, and ripped off her burning skirt. By this time, Alma was rolling in the grass, successfully putting out flames on her dress.

Smoke poured out of the door and windows of the kitchen above. When I arrived to help, Priscilla had put out the flames with the extinguisher she still held in her hand. The kitchen and house were spared.

A quick survey revealed that the one most seriously burned was Myra Lou, whom they had wrapped in a blanket to smother the flames. I couldn't tell the severity of her burns until she was examined at the clinic. Since the house was immediately adjacent, Myra insisted, "I can walk!" Off she went flanked by Lenore and me.

We removed the blanket, cut off the few remnants of her nylon clothing with bandage scissors, and placed her on fresh sheets. To my dismay, I saw that over 70 percent of her body was burned. A large proportion of the burned area was third-degree. We inserted an intravenous catheter for the electrolyte solutions she needed immediately to keep ahead of the inevitable fluid loss. Then we began the debriding and bandaging process, which took a couple of hours.

Partway through the process, Lenore realized that her burns were making her feel faint. She sank to the floor and patiently awaited her turn along with Alma and Kaye who also had less severe burns.

Attendants lifted Myra Lou onto a stretcher, wheeled her to the newly opened infirmary, and placed her in a hospital bed.

Now Lenore needed burn dressings. Her left leg was burned from hip to ankle on the outer half. I found only a couple of small patches of third-degree damage. Soon she, too, was in a bed across the hall from Myra. Then Alma and Kaye were patched up and admitted with minor wounds.

After severe and extensive burns, the first week of patient care is critical. One of Myra's arms was spared from injury so that we had access to the veins needed for infusions. She looked like a mummy, wrapped from head to toe in bandages. Her hair was singed, the left side of her face blistered, and the left ear charred. Nevertheless, her medications kept her relatively comfortable, and she got a little sleep.

In thinking through our management of her condition, I realized that if we, by God's grace, could get her through the first few weeks, Myra could be airlifted to Manila safely. Doctors there would begin skin grafting, and then she could be flown to the United States when she had stabilized. Wycliffe's Summer Institute of Linguistics (SIL) provided nurses to give round-the-clock care. One SIL nurse, Vivian Forsberg, flew down from Manila, bringing urgently needed supplies. Together with our Filipino staff nurses, they gave Myra tender loving care.

An invaluable contribution of these special-duty people was that they gave me a well- rounded picture of how Myra was doing. One of the nurses was an optimist, and her reports usually bore a cheery note of good progress; another of the nurses was a bit pessimistic, and tended to give me a darker side of the story; but the third was strictly realistic and gave me the simple facts. I couldn't rely entirely on what the patient said, for she was the most cheerful and optimistic soul I had ever encountered. She neither went into shock nor gave me a moment's anxiety.

Around the clock and around the world, friends of Myra Lou and Wycliffe comprised another chain of specialists at work: prayer partners. We were certain that her good progress could only be attributed to the fact that she was in the loving hands of her Savior and Lord.

She was also most compliant in following our medical orders.

On rounds the morning after the fire I said, "Mike (Myra Lou's nickname), we've got to get sufficient fluids, electrolytes and proteins into you orally so that we can save the few good veins you still have. We need them for the plasma that we're having flown to us. You must be on a special diet, whether it is palatable or not, okay?" "Sure, you're the Doc." And her actions were as good as her word. She had to drink volumes of eggnog until she couldn't look a hen in the beak. Her other oral fluids were laced with our own special recipe of salt, soda and sugar that would have put the Gatorade people out of business. We tried different combinations of juices to try to improve the taste, but that only ruined the fruit flavors. She got it down with a generous supply of crushed ice.

As Myra's condition stabilized over the next few days, her friends related details of the fire more clearly. Jan Forster offered her observations:

"Alma went out to the kitchen to see if the water was hot for cocoa. She discovered that the kerosene refrigerator, which she had turned off during supper, was on fire. Everyone but me piled out to the kitchen to see. I figured that the seven of them could take care of it. Someone said it was out. Then someone else said, 'No, there's still fire inside.' By then I was curious enough to walk over to the kitchen door.

"The refrigerator's kerosene tank was on the floor where Alma had dragged it, intending to throw it outside. Mike had grabbed some pot-holders and was squatting over it to try to smother the fire, and had apparently succeeded. However, just as I got to the door, the thing made like a flame thrower, erupting fire and probably kerosene through the hole where the wick attachment belongs. I made for the front door as fast as possible and yelled once for Link Nelson.

"I'm not clear on the details after that. Anyway, I turned around and saw Mike ablaze from head to foot, trying to smother the fire with the reed mat. Rosemary Ullery, an ABWE nurse, and I tried to help her, but the air could still get to the fire. Rosemary burned her hands trying to tear Mike's skirt off. Orlon-nylon will burn and melt, but it won't tear. Finally, I got the covers off Kaye's bed, and, with the Lord's help, we put out the fire."

It is a wonder no one was killed and the house didn't go up in flames. God arranged that this accident occurred at the hospital compound rather than at the Wycliffe camp. Travel by car would have taken too long to get Myra to the hospital over those terrible roads. Furthermore, the infirmary was finished and ready for occupancy that very week.

When we talked with Myra Lou, trying to bring a bit of comfort and cheer, she made the startling comment, "Don't feel sorry for me! I asked for this!"

Seeing our incredulous expressions, she explained, "While we were on vacation, during some of my private devotional times, I was reading some of the works of F.B. Meyer. As I recall, the essence of what he said was, 'If we're not willing for the Lord's perfect will in our lives, then ask him to make us willing to be willing.' So I asked the Lord for that. I asked the Lord to do something in my life." The fire, she surmised, was God's answer. And she was making the best of it.

In about three weeks Myra's burn areas had sealed over cleanly with the usual burn eschar. She had no evidence of infection and her vital signs were stable. That was the best window of opportunity for airlifting her to a burn center. Right on schedule with God's timing, the commanding officer of the Philippine Constabulary camp on the other side of town came to report that a Philippine Air Force plane would be arriving the next day to fly Myra Lou to Manila.

The hospital staff had Myra at the landing field on the edge of town when the plane landed the next morning. Before the crew lifted the stretcher aboard, we all gathered around and sang my favorite hymn, "He Leadeth Me." After a short prayer, the crew secured

Myra's stretcher to the deck, and the plane took off with Jan and Vivian accompanying her.

What should have been a four-hour flight turned into a thirteen-hour one. The plane had mechanical problems which kept it on the ground in two different cities for the extra hours. By the time it arrived in Manila, where the SIL team was awaiting her with an ambulance, the delay had set Myra Lou's temperature rising. That night it reached 106 degrees Fahrenheit. Still she insisted, "Don't feel sorry for me; I asked for this. I prayed to the Lord to purify me."

Although preparations had been made for a plane to take her to the U.S., the doctors at the American Hospital in Manila considered her condition too critical. The flight had to be canceled.

Only her unshakable faith in the Lord of her life kept her sane and content through those trying days. In her mind, what had befallen her was not "an unfortunate accident." God had permitted it.

One of her favorite quotes comes from George Keith's hymn, "How Firm a Foundation:"

"When through fiery trials thy pathway shall lie,

My grace, all sufficient, shall be thy supply;

The flame shall not hurt thee; I only design

Thy dross to consume and thy gold to refine."

Myra Lou was in the hospital in Manila for a full year, receiving donor skin grafts from missionary colleagues. She didn't have any areas of her own body that could be used as donor sites. Although donor grafts were of temporary value in stemming the loss of fluids and hastening healing, most were eventually rejected. She received 60 blood transfusions besides numerous plasma units. Only someone who has experienced this can sympathize realistically with her physical suffering.

Through it all, Myra Lou and others learned valuable lessons. One of her nurses, Vivian, wrote: "As a group, we're learning that we are members one of another; when one member suffers, we all suffer. The purifying fire Myra Lou asked for has started its work in our hearts, too."

Howard McKaughan, an SIL director wrote, "All of us, with the possible exception of Myra Lou, feel that what happened to her was for *our* sakes more than for hers, just as the apostle Paul claimed that his imprisonment resulted in the furtherance of the gospel. It has drawn us closer together in teamwork and in sensitivity to the Lord's signals."

After coming through one crisis after another in the recovery process, Myra Lou also referred to a Bible passage on the interdependence of the members of the body:

"The members of the body which seem to be weaker are necessary; and those members of the body which we think less honorable, on those we bestow more abundant honor" (1 Corinthians 12:22-23 NASB).

"It touches me deeply when I think of how the Lord's people pulled together to save my life," she continued. "Who am I that I should be given such consideration? It wasn't who I was, but my position was the weaker member. It is humbling to be indispensable because of one's helplessness."

Dr. Richard Pittman, the Philippine branch director of SIL who had spearheaded the Wycliffe work in that country, summarized it succinctly: "The teamwork galvanized by the fire was beyond anything which those of us involved in the case had ever seen before."[2]

After that year in Manila, Myra Lou was transferred to a burn center in the United States. Several more operations followed, plus physical therapy and rehabilitation.

Approximately two and a half years from the time of the fire, the inseparable sisters in the bonds of Christ, Jan and Myra Lou, alighted from a plane that brought them back to their fellow translators and their beloved Manobos of the southern Philippines.

Myra Lou's legs still required pressure bandages to aid the circulation and to protect the delicate skin. Otherwise one would hardly know she had been tried by fire. Her radiance and contentment mark her as one who has been walking close to her Lord, the Great Purifier.

Can you imagine the joy and sense of awe that this whole experience had on the Bethel staff? I refer not just to the joy of

---

[2] Atherton, William, *In God's Time and Ours,* (Manila: Summer Institute of Linguistics), p. 158

having Mike and Jan back, but the emotions that must be akin to those experienced by Mary and Martha in scripture when their brother Lazarus was restored to them. God had restored Myra Lou to health as He had raised Lazarus to life.

The amazing thing was that God had chosen to use *us* in the healing process. We were allowed to share in the teamwork that placed God's Word in understandable form in the hands of a Philippine minority culture. A vital part of medical missions is helping maintain the health of *missionaries* so that they can finish the task God has equipped them to do.

Jan and Myra Lou completed the translation of the Dibabawon New Testament and a song book of indigenous tribal tunes. They had the joy of seeing those come off the press and distributed in the tribe before their retirement in 1993.

You won't have any trouble picking out Myra Lou and Jan when you get to heaven. They'll be surrounded by Dibabawon saints singing praises to their heavenly Father!

15
TESTIMONIES FROM THE CLINIC

"Therefore if any man be in Christ, he is a new creature:
old things are passed away; behold, all things are become new"
(2 Corinthians 5:17).

JULIET

"I tried to kill myself," she testified to a congregation at Bethel
Baptist Church one Sunday evening, "but God wouldn't let me die."

Juliet had taken a handful of tablets in a desperate mood of
frustration and depression. It wasn't hard to get them. Her husband
was a physician. He had graduated from medical school in Manila,
completed his year of internship, passed the Medical Board
examinations, and had been licensed recently to practice. Since he
was a son of a prominent and respected doctor in the community, the
family was part of the upper strata of society. But the possession of
things was not satisfying to Juliet.

She awoke the morning after taking the overdose of medicine
and found she was still alive with the same problems. She doubled
the amount of pills and swallowed them with a volume of water till
she could take no more. She awoke the next morning still alive.

"Why can't I die?"

She caught a glimpse of a loaded pistol in her husband's drawer.
Placing it to her temple, she pulled the trigger. Click! No explosion.
She was sure it had been loaded.

"WHY CAN'T I DIE?!"

She decided she would just have to try again later.

Shortly thereafter, her husband applied to work at Bethel Baptist Hospital. I can remember inviting him into my office for an interview one day in December 1975.

After the usual pleasantries and data gathering, I said, "You know, Doctor, this is a mission hospital and one of our requirements is that each staff members is a born-again Christian, has invited Christ into his or her life as Savior and Lord. Each is interested in working here in order to help people in need physically and at the same time tell them of God's love. May I ask you if you know Christ as your Savior, too?"

Though he had lived in Malaybalay all his life, apart from his college years, I did not remember ever seeing him in church. He had a reputation of being involved in the usual worldly activities. So I really wasn't prepared for his reply. "Yes, I accepted Jesus as a boy in Sunday school. But I haven't really done much about it. You know, college and medical school put a lot of doubts in my mind about the Bible and Christian things. I stopped going to church. I do drink and smoke a little. But perhaps if I work here I can learn."

What impressed me was his sincerity and openness. The fact that he knew our purpose in being a missionary arm of the Baptist fellowship, helping plant and nourish churches, had not deterred him from applying. Furthermore, his parents were good friends of ours. We had been praying that they would take an open and active stand for Christ. Perhaps the Lord was answering our prayers in their son's employment application.

After talking it over with Lenore, I encouraged the medical committee to recommend to the Board of Directors of the hospital that Dr. "Boy" (his nick-name) be invited to join the staff on a trial basis. Everyone agreed and he began working in January 1976.

The Lord was obviously working in the doctor's heart. One Sunday evening, a few months later, he testified in church. He looked at me as he said, "Dr. Nelson, when I told you I was a Christian, I really wasn't sure. But tonight I can honestly tell you that Jesus Christ is my Savior!"

What joy it was to see the Lord bring that young couple and their four precious children into active involvement in the church. The pastor had a Bible study in their home every Saturday evening to help them mature in their faith.

Now, several months later, his wife Juliet was giving her testimony in church. She concluded, "God wouldn't let me die by the overdose of medicine or the loaded pistol because He wanted me for heaven and I wasn't ready. But on August 3, 1976 I knelt in my room and asked Jesus to come into my life!" Through tears of joy she told of the change that resulted and the confidence of having heaven as her future home. She pled with her relatives and friends to accept the Savior, too.

As the hospital evangelist commented, "Now they have something to live for; and something worth dying for."

What if we hadn't accepted the doctor's application? Dr. "Boy" Flores went on to become medical director of Bethel Baptist Hospital after several years on the staff. Although he later resigned and became a leader in city government and community service, he often brings his private patients that need hospitalization to Bethel.

EUNICE

The missionaries at the Hospital received this letter one day, quite early in our experience.

"Dalwangan, Malaybalay, Bukidnon
May 29, 1953

Dear Mrs. Esson,

Greeting you in the blessed Name of our Lord and Savior Jesus Christ who saved us from our sins.

Here am I, telling you about this, which I have been suffering for a long time. Maybe it is the will of God that I will suffer for this sickness, because it was the one which brought me to be near Him. If not for this sickness, I will not be able to find the Way of Salvation. How I thank the Lord for it.

Now my wound is becoming bigger again, but
I cannot go to the hospital cause I have no money for
my bus charge. I have more tablets yet, but my
sickness just become worse. It was better I think when
I was yet taking my injections. But now that the
injections are already consume, prayer is needed. I
asked for more prayers to you. God's will must be
done. I need more bandages and ten centavos plasters.
Thank you. In His most blessed Name,
Yours,
[signed] Eunice"

Her diagnosis was Hansen's Disease, better known by its older
name: *Leprosy*. Eunice was a sweet teenager living in a village about
six miles (ten kilometers) from Bethel Clinic. At that time, the only
effective treatment for leprosy, common in the tropics, was a sulfone
compound. The tablet form of the medicine was inexpensive but
very slow acting and had to be taken for the rest of the patient's life.
Although the injectable form cost more, many patients preferred to
be injected. We soon learned that many patients didn't think they
were treated for their illness unless they received an injection: *any*
injection.

Eunice had been coming to the clinic for about six months, and
her condition had already advanced. She was enjoying some
improvement, but it was slow. Her biggest expense was the bus ride,
which cost about ten cents each way in our currency. We supplied
the tablets without cost whenever she couldn't afford them. But
getting to the clinic was a hassle because of the stigma associated
with her disease. People shunned her. They were afraid to sit beside
her if they recognized the outward signs — the lumpy facial features,
the disfigured hands.

At first she stayed in a nearby cottage and came daily to the clinic
for her injection. As she gradually improved she was given the tablet
form of medication and allowed to return home.

Leprosy is now referred to as Hansen's Disease to lessen the stigma associated with the illness. In 1870, Gerhard Armauer Hansen, a Norwegian physician, first proved leprosy to be caused by a bacillus that primarily attacks the nerves that carry sensation.

The disease is as ancient as the days of Moses. God spelled out its diagnostic features to Moses and instructed him on how to care for those afflicted. There was no known cure, except for the few miracles that are recorded as in the case of Naaman, the Syrian army captain in Second Kings chapter five. Victims of the dread malady were excluded from their villages, and every attempt was made to keep them from endangering others. In the New Testament, Jesus miraculously cured ten lepers at one time, as well as individuals at other times.

In the first decade of this century, the U.S. Public Health service tried to rid the Philippines of infectious diseases. Smallpox was eventually controlled by vaccinations, and malaria was checked with quinine. But leprosy was among the especially difficult challenges. A large stone building, named San Lazaro Hospital by the Franciscan monks, had been constructed in 1784 to care for those patients, but many still wandered about the Manila streets. They were usually beggars, shunned and feared.

Health officials estimated that 10,000 to 30,000 lepers were scattered throughout the Philippines in 1900. Since there was no known remedy at that time, the first step was to isolate the patients in colonies, in order to protect the healthy members of society. You can imagine the heart-rending tales that accompanied those separations from family!

The largest of those colonies was established on the tiny island of Culion, 200 miles (320 kilometers) southwest of Manila. That island is adjacent to the island of Coron, Palawan, and is 20 miles (32 kilometers) long by 12 miles (19 kilometers) wide at its widest point. Government officials moved the few nomadic aborigines who lived on Culion to another nearby island to protect them from getting the disease.

By 1906 the colony was ready for the lepers. Boat loads of patients were transferred from a hospital in Cebu and from others on Luzon.

The Sisters of St. Paul de Chartres, a band of professionals, dedicated their lives to the care and treatment of lepers.

Through the years that followed, concern for the lepers became the special burden of Christian organizations. Dr. Victor Heiser wrote:[1]

> "Christian religious societies have always interested themselves in caring for lepers, and have been virtually the only ones who have done so. All other religions have, as a rule, held aloof. But sympathy for the afflicted, a Christian tenet, has done much to alleviate the sufferings of those unfortunate people. The American Mission to Lepers, fostered by the American churches, works in many foreign countries, particularly India."

Culion became the center for research on the treatment of Hansen's Disease. In 1907 Dr. Isadore Dyer, Professor of Dermatology at Tulane University found chaulmoogra oil to be somewhat effective in arresting the disease. So Dr. Heiser, Director of Health for the Philippines gave it a trial in Culion. Happily, after a year of treatment, several patients tested negative for the bacteria. But the search continued for more effective medicines. One of the more famous of the researchers, Dr. H. Windsor Wade, transferred to Culion from the pathology department of the University of the Philippines. That important step was taken when Leonard Wood was Governor General.

Governor General Wood's concern for the lepers was eventually rewarded in that donations from America funded the erection of a new laboratory in Culion and a new hospital in Cebu as part of the Leonard Wood Memorial for the Eradication of Leprosy. Specialists in the research and care of leprosy came from all over the world to a Leonard Wood Memorial Conference on Leprosy at Manila in January 1931. Before long, an international activity subsidized by the Memorial was the International Leprosy Association and its publication, *The International Journal of Leprosy*, the latter edited by Dr. Wade.

In time, newer medications were discovered for the treatment of leprosy. No longer are patients required to be isolated in colonies,

---

[1] Heiser, Dr. Victor, *An American Doctor's Odyssey,* W.W. Norton & Co., Inc., pg. 255

and as long as they are under a physician's care and receiving the right medicine they can live at home. Of course, the patients and family members are instructed in hygienic measures that must be followed. Nevertheless, the stigma of Hansen's Disease lingers. Some patients who have been free of the disease for years still prefer to remain in the colonies because residual scars betray their past illness.

Let's get back to the story of Eunice, our patient at the Bethel Baptist Clinic in Malaybalay. The routine at the ABWE mission clinic was that patients would be seen each morning, except for Wednesdays and Sundays, beginning at 7:30. Just prior to the doors being opened, one of us missionaries, or later a clinic chaplain, would present a short gospel service with the waiting patients. They knew the system: first come, first served. Some would come before dawn in order to get the front seats. On many clinic days, about 100 patients came, together with their companions, making quite a sizeable congregation. The clinic chaplain would present the simple plan of salvation, using Bible stories and sometimes object lessons.

For what shall it profit a man, if he shall gain the whole world [*including a healthy body*], and lose his own soul? Or what shall a man give in exchange for his soul? (Mark 8:36-37).

Some call this method Holistic Medicine: we spell it *wholistic*. In treating sick patients, we must consider their physical, emotional and spiritual needs. Each aspect of the person is involved, so the *whole* person should be treated. Through the years, some have complained that this is "forcing religion down the throats" of patients. They claim that we are taking advantage of sick people by "proselytizing" them.

To the contrary, this approach gives the *thinking* patient an opportunity to realize that his make-up is more than physical. And God wants everyone, regardless of race, to invite Christ into his life and restore a healthy relationship with God who created man in His own image.

Noted theologian, Dr. J. Sidlow Baxter, describes it this way: "To be created 'in the image of God' means not only that we are body, mind, and spirit but that we are *capas Dei* ("capable of God"). The lower animals are body and mind, but not spirit; therefore, they have neither capacity *for*, nor consciousness *of* God. Critical psychological investigation finds that in even primitive aboriginals that deep-down consciousness of God is present. It may be idolatrously perverted or indistinctly dormant, but it is there, ineradicably so. The *pneuma* or spirit may be defunct, yet in one way or another it cries out for the true God. That constitutional consciousness of God gives the knock-out blow to the evolution theory. Mind and spirit simply cannot evolve from matter. Man is unique and precious to God."

Mankind is on a much higher level of creation than the animals, who lack a God consciousness. Man certainly has not evolved from these lower forms of life. Rather, he is God's masterpiece of creation. It takes more faith to believe in the unproven theory of evolution than it does to believe in an intelligent, all powerful Master-builder.

The problem is that mankind, because of these unique qualities and characteristics, has the ability to make choices. God gave men and women volition: a free will. Man is not a robot. The enemy of God, called Satan or the devil, himself a unique and powerful mind, opposes all that is of God and influences men and women to make the wrong choices. That began back in the Garden of Eden when the serpent spoke with Eve:

> Yea, hath God said, Ye shall not eat of every tree of the garden? ... Ye shall not surely die: for God doth know that in the day ye eat thereof, then your eyes shall be opened, and ye shall be as gods, knowing good and evil (Genesis 3:1,4,5).

Eve *chose* to disobey God. In so doing she sinned and then chose to involve Adam, her husband, to do the same. God judged them both and expelled them from the garden. Since then, men and women have had to consciously and individually choose to obey God or to obey Satan.

In Cebuano, the language spoken by the majority of the people in the southern half of the Philippines, the word for *leprosy* and the word for *sin* are very nearly the same: *sanla* and *sala*, respectively. Just one letter makes the difference.

The comparison of the two conditions makes an interesting study. The patient with leprosy may not realize he is a victim of the disease for a long time. It starts out quite inconspicuously, perhaps with a single skin lesion on the scalp. Nevertheless, it is in his blood and will eventually become manifest to all. Furthermore, medicine may arrest the progress of symptoms without curing the disease. Eventually, it leads to death. The same is true of sin: "The soul that sinneth ... shall die" (Ezekiel 18:4b).   The analogy of leprosy and sin differs, however, in that there is a *cure* for sin:

> The wages of sin is death; but the gift of God is eternal life through Jesus Christ our Lord (Romans 6:23).
>
> Neither is there salvation in any other: for there is none other name under heaven given among men, whereby we must be saved (Acts 4:12).
>
> Choose you this day whom ye will serve, ... but as for me and my house, *we will serve the Lord"* (Joshua 24:15).

Eunice heard this explanation of the origin of sin and made her choice to invite Christ into her life. As she mused later, if it had not been for her illness, she might not have heard the truth about herself and about the way back to fellowship with God.

So she *thanked* God for leprosy! Though we have lost track of Eunice, we are confident that we shall meet in God's heavenly home.

MELODY

Melody lived near the city of Cagayan de Oro, or thereabouts. As a teenager she was sent to "get a number" at the Bethel Baptist Clinic. The way an adult could get around the requirement that patients attend the pre-clinic gospel service was to send a child or a servant ahead to get a front seat. The low-numbered tag that went with that seat indicated the order of being seen by the doctor. Then the real patient would show up later when the service was concluded and take the child's appointment number. Melody may have rebelled at the inconvenience of getting up early, catching a bus and sitting through the service. But she did so out of love for her parents.

Her parent's illness required repeated visits. Melody seemed to be the one who had to sit through the services most of the time. The good news being preached began to stir her heart. The Lord also sent a Christian schoolmate to be a close friend. Before long, Melody asked Jesus into her life. In time she learned more and more about her new-found faith as she attended a nearby Baptist church. She was influenced by a discerning pastor to attend Bible school. Later she went off to Doane Baptist Bible Institute (DBBI).

At DBBI Melody and Pete became friends. After graduation and a few years of practical experience in churches, they teamed up as husband and wife and applied to the *Philippine Association of Baptists for World Evangelism (PABWE)*[2]. Mr. and Mrs. Pete Wong became missionaries to Thailand where they ministered for years, doing a commendable work for their Lord.

Little did we know what the custom of "getting a number" at Bethel Baptist Clinic might bring forth. But we're so glad for what resulted in the life of Pete and Melody Wong.

RUBY

By 1985 the Bukidnon ministry was fully autonomous. The last of ABWE's missionaries in Bukidnon, Dave and Becky Nelson and their children, moved their base of operation to the developing ABWE outreach in Leyte. The Bukidnon ministries have flourished under national leadership. A newsletter from Malaybalay emphasized the fact that the hospital was continuing with the same goals, principles and practices. The letter recorded another beautiful example of the importance of treating the whole person.

"Bethel Baptist Hospital
October 1993
8700 Malaybalay, Bukidnon, Philippines

[2] Appendix I

144

Dear Dr. Link and Mrs. Nelson,

We just had our supper when the phone rang. It was a long distance call and on the other end of the line was a pleasant woman whom we had not heard from for several months. Ruby sounded happy, confident, and at peace — with no trace of the fear and suspicion that characterized her voice before. She told us she's now in school and is presently staying with her relatives.

Ruby's call brought back memories of the evening when she was first brought to the hospital. She looked pale and haggard, unable to sleep, panting, and with severe chest pain. She was still in her late teens, but her life was already wrecked by almost four years of rugged, spartan living as a fugitive in the mountains, forsaken even by her family. At that time she was a Communist hit-squad leader sent to our town by their commander to assassinate one of the military informers. She had done this assignment several times before. She was noted to be one of the reliable and effective assassins in their group. As before, any failure on her part would have meant her own death.

She had two opportunities to carry out this latest job. But in both instances her increasingly troubled conscience stopped her. She still had not carried out her assignment when she was brought to us. At that time, another team was sent to check on her as to why she hadn't reported back. Her hospitalization had given her an alibi to postpone her work. That allowed her to buy time and to reflect about her life and future.

There was nothing medically wrong with her on examination. Her fears and guilt weighed down heavily on her: mentally, physically, emotionally and spiritually. In confidence she told her deep desire to leave the rebel movement and to lead a quiet and peaceful life.

In the hospital she learned of God's great love for her. She had never experienced true love. She only knew how it was to be used as a tool, exploited by a cause that bred hatred and fear. She learned, too, that Christ came and paid the penalty due to her sins by His atoning death on the cross. Also that He was willing and able to forgive her and to give her the peaceful and secure life that she desired. She had heard of Christ as a young girl but she had never realized that Christ loved her personally and that He could deliver her from all her fears and guilt. For Ruby it was an awesome and overwhelming truth! With tears in her eyes, she surrendered her life to Jesus as her Savior and Lord.

Ruby is just one of the countless lives that God has touched and made whole in the hospital. We praise Him for the privilege of allowing us to experience the mighty deeds He is doing in our midst.
By His Grace,
[signed] Allan & Blessie"

Allan Melicor was the surgeon who worked with us at Bethel Hospital for several years prior to our retirement. He had passed the examinations and was accepted as a diplomat of the Philippine College of Surgeons. He married a charming Christian, named Blessie, a licensed veterinarian. Their professional expertise and spiritual leadership were valuable assets in the ministry of the hospital.

Juliet, Eunice, Melody, and Ruby, along with a host of other patients, found new life at Bethel Baptist Hospital. How well they demonstrate the truth of 2 Corinthians 5:17:

> Therefore if any man be in Christ, he is a new creature:
> old things are passed away; behold, all things are
> become new.

16
DOCTOR TONY

"And Jesus said unto them, Ye will surely say unto me this proverb,
Physician, heal thyself " (Luke 4:23).

Tony was a dear friend and colleague. His full name was Antonio
Maravilla, M.D. He was born on March 27, 1927 in the province of
Negros Occidental, which is in the central group of islands of the
Philippines known as the Visayas.

He grew up in the town of Su-ay, Himamaylan, the youngest of
five brothers and two sisters. Early in his youth, he invited Christ
into his life. His education took him through college and then medical
school at the University of Santo Tomas in Manila.

After graduation and licensure, he practiced medicine for a while
in his home town. Tuberculosis slowed him down for two years,
giving him time to ponder his future. He knew God had enabled him
to get that expensive professional education in order to serve the
Lord by helping his fellow-countrymen. He wondered what special
work God had for him to do.

While attending one of the biennial conferences of the Association
of Fundamental Baptist Churches in the Philippines[1] in Baguio City,
Tony heard our report of the on-going ministry of Bethel Baptist
Hospital. He was challenged immediately when we mentioned the
need for a Filipino physician to join us in the work. After that meeting,
he approached us and we were introduced. He reviewed his
background and said he would be praying for the Lord's guidance in
this new challenge.

---

[1] Appendix H

When the hospital extended a call to him to become a full-time member of the staff in Malaybalay, he accepted. In 1963 he became the first Filipino doctor to assist me in the medical work. Tony was an answer to prayer. The work was getting heavier and for ten years I had been the only doctor in the hospital except for Dr. Ed Glazier who took my place during my year of furlough.

With the arrival of Dr. Maravilla, our goal seemed within reach: qualified Christian *Filipino* doctors assuming responsibility for the hospital. Our aim was for the entire administration to be in capable Filipino hands, carrying on the policies of the mission.

None of us missionaries had experience in starting a hospital. The development of Bethel Clinic was a matter of doing what seemed right, under the guidance of the regional field council. Consultation with our mission headquarters was difficult, since 12,000 miles separated us. Some time prior to Dr. Maravilla's arrival, the medical staff developed a chart for the management of the hospital. This was designed to safeguard the purpose of its existence. We formulated the organizational chain-of-command. The simple design looked like this:

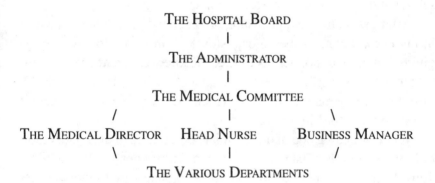

The simplicity of that arrangement probably accounted for its effectiveness. As time went on and the hospital grew, minor changes could be made without a lot of adjustment. Furthermore, when the time eventually came for the hospital to be recognized by the national government, we could document such a structure.

And government regulations *did* come along in due time. At first the requirements were rather minimal. For instance, we did not have to register as a hospital unless we had ten or more hospital beds in the in-patient department. That gave us a loop-hole to avoid the jurisdiction of the Bureau of Hospitals in Manila.

We kept our infirmary at a level of *nine* hospital beds for several years, which kept our official paper-work at a minimum. However, the regulation was changed: a private clinic with even one or two hospital beds was considered an institution that must register as a hospital; the red tape increased.

We were delighted to have Dr. Maravilla on staff. He soon was called Doctor Tony or Doctor Mar by all of us. His patients loved his quiet and unassuming manner as he cared for them. His confidence grew as he assisted me in surgery and eventually was capable of performing most operations without my supervision. The administration gave him more staff responsibilities.

In 1966 the hospital board appointed Doctor Tony as the first Filipino medical director of Bethel Baptist Hospital. That coincided with our departure on a regular furlough. An older doctor friend in town, Dr. Flores, Senior, who was very sympathetic to the purpose and work of the hospital, agreed to be a consultant for Dr. Maravilla, should he need one.

Dr. Tony developed an interest in one of the staff nurses. That romance blossomed, and when he eventually proposed marriage, Diana accepted. But getting married in the Philippines is complicated. The two families involved must be consulted, and their consent obtained. It seems to be a rule that one or more of the relatives disapprove for a while to make things a bit tense. Approval was granted finally, and the marriage took place in the bride's hometown, Bacolod City, in February 1968.

Then the testing times began. Tony came to me one morning and said he was having symptoms of amoebic dysentery, a common complaint in third world countries. Usually the parasite is passed through drinking water or contaminated vegetables which are eaten uncooked. Malaybalay lacked an efficient purification system for the drinking water.

As a precaution, we advised everyone to boil the water for fifteen minutes before cooling it for drinking. This became a rather hard and fast rule for our family. There are other ways of treating water, such as passing it through a good filter, but boiling is the safest way.

When Peace Corps volunteers are sent to the tropics, their medical coordinators stress care in eating uncooked vegetables as well. Their rule is: "Peel it, boil it, or skip it!" That makes good sense, because infected food handlers can pass along the parasite if they prepare fresh fruits and vegetables with unclean hands.

But when I examined Dr. Maravilla in July 1968 he did not have amoeba as the cause for his intestinal problem. Rather, the sigmoidoscope revealed a mass in the lower colon. It had the appearance of cancer.

What should we do? First of all, it was wise to get further laboratory tests and to repeat the biopsy. At that time, whenever we did biopsies at our hospital, we sent the specimens to the city of Cebu for laboratory tests. It took an average of two weeks or longer to get a report from the pathologist. Furthermore, I felt it would not be appropriate to operate on Tony in our small rural hospital, though we had done the procedure on other patients.

Therefore, we decided to take Dr. Maravilla to St. Luke's Hospital in Manila where I had courtesy staff privileges. There we would have the benefit of the larger facility, better equipped operating room, and the assistance of a senior surgeon and friend, Dr. Charles Harn. The laboratory would also be able to give reports on the biopsy and other tests within a few hours.

The first operation in July of 1968 went well and the malignant segment of colon was resected. Tony's recovery was uncomplicated. He was out of the hospital after two weeks and back to work on a limited basis within a month or so.

But the cancer recurred. I arranged for surgical consultation in Santa Barbara, California, where I had been a resident in surgery and was especially confident in the expertise of my former proctors. So Tony and Diana, who was pregnant at the time, flew to California and Tony had to undergo a more radical operation in December 1968. A couple months later they were able to return to the Philippines.

Diana's concern for Tony and the travel involved had been difficult for her. In the spring of 1969, Mrs. Maravilla delivered prematurely. Their baby weighed only two pounds ten ounces! They named her Dawn. God spared her life and she gradually gained weight and developed into a lively, healthy child. Dawn was the joy of her daddy's heart.

Getting used to a colostomy wasn't easy for Doctor Tony, but he had the courage and determination to conquer his problem. Several months passed before he could return to part-time work at the hospital. He resumed his directorship, witnessed the growth of Bethel Baptist Hospital and participated in the dedication of the new surgical building in April 1971.

That dedication was memorable. For one thing, the new addition was named in his honor: the Maravilla Surgical Wing. Prominent people attended the dedication: the governor of the province and his retinue, the mayor of Malaybalay and his aides, representatives from civic organizations and mission agencies such as the Summer Institute of Linguistics, and the official representative of ABWE, Russell Ebersole, Jr, then Executive Administrator for the Far East.

Russ gave the main address at the dedication. He told the story of the "detour" by which he had come to the ceremony: he and his wife Nancy were on their way to Mindanao a few days ahead of the scheduled dedication. They had planned to stop in Davao first to meet with ABWE personnel who worked in that southern-most province. But after their plane had been airborne a few minutes out of Manila, a group of university students with communist leanings high-jacked the flight and forced the pilot to head for mainland China. The pilot explained that he didn't have enough fuel to go that far, but that he could reach Hong Kong. After considerable haggling, they allowed him to refuel in Hong Kong and then proceed to Canton, China.

The passengers were kept in military barracks overnight, not certain of their fate. But the next day they were finally released. The plane and the passengers returned to Manila. The highjackers remained in China.

You can imagine the tense moments they had endured! Mrs. Ebersole was especially concerned about their seven children left in Manila while they were on that frightful trip. Of course, it was a prominent news item being broadcast on the radio and on TV. When they finally landed in Manila, Russ was ready to continue on to the appointments in Mindanao, but Nancy opted for recuperating at home with their household. Russ, nevertheless, felt he should be at the dedication and took the next flight south, arriving in Malaybalay the day of the program.

The audience was spellbound by Russ's tale of God's deliverance and of God's faithfulness to His children under extreme pressures. He also related how at least one of his fellow captives, an executive of a major pharmaceutical company, put his trust in the Lord as he listened to Russ's witness while on that flight. That was a message Dr. Tony needed to hear, for he, too, was on a perilous journey with recurrent cancer.

Several months later, the Philippine Hospital Association presented a trophy to the Bethel Baptist Hospital during National Hospital week in May 1972. We were out of the country on furlough. Doctor Tony was unable personally to accept the award because he was once again confined to a hospital bed; his symptoms had recurred. His wife, Diana, however, went to Manila as representative of the hospital and received the trophy, giving witness to the faithfulness of the God of Bethel.

We booked a flight back to the Philippines as soon as school vacation began. Soon after landing in Manila on July 22, 1972, we learned that our beloved physician, Antonio Maravilla, had died the day before at just 45 years of age.

A few days later, we returned to Malaybalay by way of Su-ay, on the island of Negros Occidental in order to participate in the funeral of our dear friend. The entire village, it seemed, walked in the procession behind the carriage which carried his coffin. The week before his funeral and every year thereafter on the date of Tony's death, special evangelistic services were held in the yard of the Maravilla homestead, urging town-mates to trust in the Savior whom Doctor Maravilla had loved and served. He was a beloved physician, indeed.

The loss of Doctor Tony was a blow to his wife and to all of us who had worked with him at Bethel Baptist Hospital. Our confidence that Dr. Tony was God's answer for that planned turn-over of the hospital to national leadership collapsed. The time table for establishing an autonomous medical facility was postponed for want of someone with his quality of leadership.

Such times of bereavement and disappointment make us wonder, *"Where is God in these hurts?"*

Many had prayed earnestly for Tony that he would be healed of his cancer. Wasn't God listening? Certainly He is able to heal. Wasn't He willing? Doesn't the Bible state that by Jesus wounds we are healed (1 Peter 2:24)? Was our faith too weak? Isn't Christ the same yesterday, and today, and forever, as the Bible states in Hebrews 13:8? Certainly earthly parents would not permit a need to persist in their child if they had the power to relieve it, would they? Isn't our Heavenly Father concerned about happiness?

Perhaps it would be more appropriate to ask, "Are there Biblical reasons for our *not* being healed today?" Gratefully, an answer has been given by another highly respected and astute Bible scholar and theologian, Dr. J. I. Packer. He addressed a gathering of medical professionals and students under the auspices of the Christian Medical and Dental Society in 1983. From the audiotapes of this seminar, made available by Covenant Distributors (P.O. Box 14488, Augusta, GA 30919), I have gleaned some helpful insights.

Dr. Packer states that it is destructive -- and, in fact, a fallacy -- to tell an invalid or one suffering from something like cancer that he is not well *because of his lack of faith.* Our heavenly Father, in His sovereignty, is more concerned with our eternal *holiness* than He is with our earthly *happiness.* He is primarily preparing us for heaven — the long-term outlook. In the process, discipline may be one of His options (Hebrews 12). As the apostle Paul wrote in Romans

9:21,

> Hath not the potter power over the clay, of the same lump
> to make one vessel unto honour, and another unto
> dishonour?

The will of a sovereign God is not ours to question. Nor are we able to find all the answers while in this life. We must trust His judgment as to what is best for us finite mortals in this process of preparing us for His heavenly home. Then, and then only, will we be given perfect bodies like Christ has right now in heaven, bodies that are not limited by illness and handicaps, nor subject to sin and decay.

Paul, of all people, could certainly speak to such an argument. He was a man of faith and at times was able to heal the sick and exorcize evil spirits from sufferers. However, not everyone was healed by Paul miraculously, as illustrated in the lives of people such as Timothy, Trophemus and Epaphroditus. And when he himself was afflicted with a physical impairment (possibly a painful eye disease), his thrice pled prayers were answered contrary to his desire. God let him know that he would *not* be relieved of this painful chronic illness, to guard him against *pride* in having had that vision of heaven:

> And He said unto me, My grace is sufficient for thee: for
> my strength is made perfect in weakness. Most gladly
> therefore will I rather glory in my infirmities, that the power
> of Christ may rest upon me (2 Corinthians 12:9).

Since Jesus miraculously healed the blind, the deaf, the chronically ill paralytic, and even raised the dead, why isn't He continuing this work on the same scale today? Dr. Packer answers that we must remember that the healings of Jesus were *signs* which authenticated His being who He claimed to be: the Son of God.

> And many other *signs* truly did Jesus in the presence of his
> disciples, which are not written in this book: but these are
> written, that ye might believe that Jesus is the Christ, the
> Son of God; and that believing ye might have life through
> his name (John 20:30-31).

And when John the Baptist sent his disciples to ask Jesus, "Art thou he that should come? or look we for another?" Jesus replied, "Go your way, and tell John what things ye have seen and heard:

how that the blind see, the lame walk, the lepers are cleansed, the deaf hear, the dead are raised, to the poor the gospel is preached" (Luke 7:19, 22). In so doing, Jesus was affirming that He was indeed the Messiah. His miracles were the exact fulfillment of the prophecy recorded in Isaiah 61 which described what to look for in the Messiah who would come.

Do we still need such *signs* to know who Jesus is? Of course not. The completed scriptures give ample evidence of His deity and Messiah-ship. Now our part is to exhibit an unconditional *faith* in Him, "Whom having not seen, ye love; in whom, though now ye see him not, yet believing, ye rejoice with joy unspeakable and full of glory; receiving the end of your faith, even the salvation of your souls" (1 Peter 1:8-9). So then faith cometh by hearing, and hearing by the *Word of God* (Romans 10:17).

God still heals today. Every honest physician and surgeon will confess that wounds and illnesses are often healed in ways we cannot explain. Sometimes the doctor, having advised the loved ones that there is nothing more he can do for the patient, is dumb-founded by a complete recovery of the supposedly terminally ill person. As one surgeon put it, "I can make the wound, but it takes God to heal it!"

So, Dr. Packer, I agree with you. Healing is not *always* God's will for us. As you said, "Living in an unhealed body may further our spiritual health, protecting us from the temptations of sin all around us, and strengthening us in another way which we could not have expected." Accepting ill health from God can be a spiritual milestone.

Is that not what the apostle Paul experienced? Or Joni Eareckson Tada? Or Dr. Tony Maravilla, my beloved physician and friend?

17

AND WHO IS MY NEIGHBOR?

"And he answering said, Thou shalt love the Lord thy God with all thy
heart, and with all thy soul, and with all thy strength,
and with all thy mind; and thy neighbor as thyself...
But he, willing to justify himself, said unto Jesus,
And who is my neighbor?" (Luke 10:27, 29).

Almost every church-goer knows the story about the good
Samaritan. However, its application in the life of one of our Filipino
friends will be new to you. I'd like to tell Rich's story.

Rich (short for Richfield) was born into the Cudal family, the last
of 16 children. His parents weren't well-to-do, except in children.
The salary of a school teacher wasn't much in pre-World War II days.
Several of the older children became school teachers, too. The eldest
son became a politician and was elected to a municipal office. As the
youngest, Rich was somewhat spoiled by his family.

His parents were among the first in their town to accept the
Christian faith. They joined the Baptist church in Malaybalay. They
faithfully brought up their children and taught them Christian doctrine
and values as found in the scriptures and as preached from the pulpit
by the missionary pastor, Henry deVries.

Then came the invasion of the Japanese in late December 1941.
The island of Mindanao, though 500 miles (800 kilometers) from
Manila, did not escape the hardships of life under the enemy forces.
The few Americans who lived in Malaybalay evacuated, trying to
avoid capture by the Japanese. Those that fled to a remote village

near Kitunglad mountain eventually left the Philippines by submarine. Their Navy rescuers took them to Australia. However, the deVries family was not as fortunate; they spent about four years in prison camps.

The Japanese set up their regional headquarters in the deVries' house on the property of the Baptist mission on the edge of Malaybalay. Since the Filipinos were friendly to the Americans, the Japanese considered them potential collaborators, so they were especially ruthless and cruel without provocation.

To escape the atrocities, Rich's parents packed up as much of their provisions as they could carry and fled into the forest. They found refuge among the Manobo tribal people living along the Salug River. The Cudals brought along salt and food, which were luxuries during the war years. Probably that was why they were admitted by the tribe.

But when their food ran out and they had to live off the land, their welcome wore thin. One night Rich's father was murdered while the family was sleeping on the split bamboo floor of their nipa palm house. The attacker simply slipped under their hut which was elevated four feet off the ground on stilt-like posts. Through the slits in the flooring he could determine where Rich's father was sleeping, and thrust him through with a spear.

The family fled for their lives. Rich's mother took her brood out of that area and found refuge elsewhere until the war ended. Eventually they returned to Malaybalay and rebuilt their home on their family property. Ten years later, we moved into the house vacated by the deVrieses, and soon became acquainted with the Cudal family.

By then Rich was a promising young man. He was a leader in the church's youth group and a well respected student in the local high school. He worked at odd jobs at the mission compound on Saturdays and helped around the clinic whenever he could. When he graduated from high school he was convinced that he should attend Doane Baptist Bible Institute.

Rich made good progress in his studies at Doane and graduated from the pastor's course. Several churches took interest in him, and he received invitations to candidate in churches needing a pastor. However, in his last year of training, Rich had become convinced that the Lord wanted him to become a missionary, rather than a pastor, so he declined those church opportunities.

When asked why he had made that decision, he replied, "I must return to Bukidnon. Tribal people in the mountains there have not heard the gospel. I must go back to the Manobos who killed my father and tell them about the love of Jesus."

About the same time, the Summer Institute of Linguistics (SIL), and ABWE sought ways to penetrate Manobo-land with the gospel. Dick Elkins with SIL and Ron Esson with ABWE teamed up to survey the tribal area. Establishing a good rapport with the local people seemed elusive, until Rich came along and lived among them.

Although the trip home was about a day's journey, Rich periodically visited his family. His report of progress among the Manobos was always a blessing to his supporting home church. He usually traveled by horseback since roads were not developed to the point that vehicles could drive that far interior.

One day he appeared in the emergency room at the mission hospital. He had been injured on the trail and had a deep knife wound in his lower left abdomen. We rushed him into surgery and explored the lower abdomen to determine the extent of his injuries. After making the necessary repairs, I closed the wound.

Of course, we were concerned as to how Rich was wounded. Had the Manobos tried to kill him as they had his father? Rich was a bit embarrassed to tell the story. Finally he explained that he had been using his hunting knife on the trail. He mounted his horse with the knife still unsheathed and as he was returning the knife to its sheathe on the left side of his belt, the horse balked. The knife missed the sheathe by a few inches and punctured his abdomen. We admonished him to take care or the next time he might accidentally perform his own appendectomy — without anesthesia.

The work in Manobo-land was hard on him in other ways, too. Rich had a flare-up of tuberculosis which kept him from working at full capacity for quite a while. But he responded to several months of treatment. (Tuberculosis is still among the ten most common causes of death in the Philippines.)

God blessed Rich's ministry. Today several Baptist churches stand as testimony of God's grace in Manobo-land. SIL linguists have translated the Bible into the Manobo dialect. Literacy experts have taught many of the Manobos to read. Some of their most promising young men have attended a Bible school near Malaybalay. Rich's life made a major impact on the lives of those people whom others would call his enemies, considering what they had done to his father. But no: God had impressed Rich with the fact that this tribe was his *"neighbor."*

I will not forget what it meant to trek the mountains of Bukidnon, visiting those remote Manobo villages. Toward the end of our first term, I wrote home about one such experience:

"At 9 in the morning three of us men started off for the hills: Orlan Wilhite, Carrell Aagard and I. The Lord gave us excellent weather for hiking. We didn't get caught in any appreciable rain for the four days we were out. The first leg of the hike was to the *barrio* of Kibalabag which took us six hours to reach. The trail took us across the river several times and then up a hill — which seemed to us akin to Mount Everest. You never saw such breathless white men as we were.

The pastor met us enthusiastically and his good wife had a basin of warm water to soak our feet in — all three pairs. As we changed into dry clothes in a closet-like room we could feel the eyes of the many kids peeking through the slats, but we didn't care at that stage. We ate the lunch we had brought sitting on the living room floor while the *barrio* folks squatted silently to observe our technique. That evening after having had a little rest, we held a meeting in the church. I spoke in Visayan and the pastor translated it.

That night we had supper about 8:30. I was appointed chef of the can opener and managed to get the wieners heated. Along with rice and beans, everything tasted great. But then we had to sling the hammocks. If we thought we had curious eyes on us before, this was more of a treat. Finally, we managed to get to sleep. Eyes were still upon us the next morning when Orlan dropped out of the hammock in his shorts.

It took four hours of hiking over muddy mountain trails to reach the second *barrio*. But it was a beautiful hike. Wild flowers and vines and ferns bloomed in profusion. We had good-natured carriers. They were very patient with us while we took frequent breathers and drank from the canteens. We finally puffed up the worst of the hills and found a bench with a sign in the dialect quoting Matthew 11:28: '*Come unto me, all ye that labor and are heavy laden,*'. How appropriate!

At times we had only a foot of walking space between the cliff wall on one side and the steep drop-off on the other. After a four-hour hike, we finally reached the second village named Manalog. Again the *barrio* folk were present to meet us. They extended their hands in greetings and we used them to help pull us up the last grade. We were escorted to the unoccupied house of the school teacher and before long had a bite to eat. The only difference in that place was that there were more watchers since the house was more spacious.

After a siesta we visited in the village and held an outdoor clinic session (as we did in each of the places we stopped). Before we knew it, it was time for the evening service. The church was packed. It was a delight to greet them and present the Word of God. Each of the *barrios* we visited has a Baptist church already and a fine pastor to lead the flock, so the messages were more of a devotional nature. That second *barrio* has about 90% believers now.

The evening meal of fried chicken prepared by the pastor followed and was really delicious. He is one of the lads who was trained in the one-year course in Malaybalay this last year. Then came the business of going to bed. The story was about the same as before, and we were off to sleep. Then (*bang!*) the rope at the head of my hammock broke and I dropped a couple of feet onto my back, knocking the wind out of me with a crowing noise. This brought the neighbors running to see what had happened. Before long the situation was in hand and peace settled until morning. When Orlan slipped to the floor, again the squatting visitors were ready. He got into his trousers as though it wasn't at all unusual to have strange people watching him do so.

After our time of devotions with the folks, we were about to leave when the pastor handed me an envelope: they had taken a "love offering" for their missionaries who had "suffered" to visit them! We didn't know what to say or what to do but finally took it. Later when it was counted, it amounted to ten pesos (five dollars). What a sacrifice that means on their part! We'll put the money into the Bukidnon evangelistic fund. But this puts many big churches to shame when it comes to the spirit of giving.

So off we went *down* the trail, slipping and stumbling, trying to keep up with our rugged guides. Finally at the foot of the mountain we came to the river. Again we crossed it many times against a swift mountain current. The water was about up to our thighs. Though I watched my footing, my feet went downstream faster than the rest of me, and I went in up to my ears — with two cameras in my hands held just far enough out of the water to keep them from getting wet. One of the guides downstream rescued me as I was floating by. What a laugh!

We finally came to the place where we left the river and climbed the last mountain to the third *barrio*. The view from the top was fantastic as we looked over the Bukidnon plateau far away to the west. The neat village was at our feet to the right and we could see the tiny figures waving a welcome to us. Soon we were with them and had another time of similar blessed fellowship. The hike to Buntungon had taken us four hours. That night the hammock didn't break.

Friday we were up and getting ready before daylight. The longest and hardest hike was between us and home. So off we went, with the added precaution to have a *carabao* (water buffalo) with us for riding purposes if needed. And needed he was. We each took turns at riding up one of the mountains. All went well. Eight hours later, we finally reached our destination. Our wonderful trip was completed!"

Has the gospel made a difference in those remote areas? You can be sure it has. Some of those *barrios* were notorious for violence and murder. The provincial police encouraged evangelists such as Rich to continue their work among the mountain villages because that made their job much easier. Peace and order returned to the *barrios* they had evangelized, and the killings stopped.

As we review that Biblical account of the Good Samaritan, we realize that he was a man who was willing to be involved in a cross-cultural situation, too. His race and the Jewish people were considered enemies, "for the Jews have no dealings with the Samaritans" (John 4:9). Jesus removed that racial barrier long ago. Now His followers must do the same. Along this theme, the apostle Paul wrote in Ephesians 2:11-16:

> Wherefore remember, that ye being in time past Gentiles in the flesh ... were without Christ, being aliens from the commonwealth

ofIsrael,and strangers from the covenants of promise,having no hope, and without God in the world: but now in Christ Jesus ye who sometimes were far off are made nigh by the blood of Christ. For he is our peace, who hath made both one, and hath broken down the middle wall of partition between us; having abolished in his flesh the enmity, even the law of commandments contained in ordinances; for to make in himself of twain one new man, so making peace; and that he might reconcile both unto God in one body by the cross, having slain the enmity thereby.

Of course, that type of neighborliness can be costly. It cost the Samaritan his time, physical strength, inconvenience, and even finances to go to his "enemy" with compassionate care. It cost Jesus His home in heaven, the limitations of a human body, the disrespect of His earthly half-brothers, the hatred by religious zealots, and the ultimate in sacrifice for His enemies: His very life! That is cross-cultural evangelism. And such is the heart of missions.

When others came to continue the work with that tribe, Rich was able to move on to another remote mission field: Thailand. He and his wife were accepted as missionaries with the newly formed Philippine Association of Baptists for World Evangelism (PABWE)[1]. This meant that they would learn a distinctly different language, live in an unfamiliar Asian culture, and be separated from their homeland, across the South China Sea.

PABWE was conceived in the city of Tagum, Davao in 1964 during the biennial conference of the Association of Fundamental Baptist Churches of the Philippines (AFBCP).[2] Teams of Filipino missionaries have served in Thailand ever since. Their financial support comes from the churches of the AFBCP, for the most part. What joy that gave us to see a daughter foreign mission society come into being! Several of the missionary families serving in Thailand under PABWE such as Rich and his wife have come from Bukidnon.

So, "Who is *my* neighbor?" He is anyon e-- whatever his race, color, or creed -- who needs the love and compassion which I, a servant of Jesus Christ, can give.

[1] Appendix I
[2] Appendix H

18
WEARY, YET PURSUING

"And Gideon came to Jordon and passed over,
he, and the three hundred men that were with him,
faint, yet pursuing" (Judges 8:4).

Gideon has always impressed me. He's among my heroes in the Old Testament. He obeyed the Lord, though he didn't feel up to the assigned task, especially when his forces were reduced to so few. And then he was told to surround the sleeping enemy carrying trumpets and flickering candles concealed in clay pitchers. What kind of warfare is that? *But he obeyed.* And the enemy was defeated. The Israelites were exhausted in the mopping up process, but pursued until the job was done.

Then there was Caleb. History records the reason for his victory: "because he followed the Lord God of Israel fully" (Joshua 14:14). That word of testimony not only came from his own lips (14: 8), but his commander, Moses, declared the same (14:9). Furthermore, God Himself said of Caleb, "... to Caleb will I give the land that he hath trodden upon, and to his children, because he hath wholly followed the Lord" (Deuteronomy 1:36).

He was 85 years old at the time of his greatest victory. His famous words ring in my heart: "Now therefore *give me this mountain,* whereof the Lord spoke in that day" (Joshua 14:12). Apparently Caleb didn't know that you are expected to retire long before reaching that age!

Lenore and I retired in the summer of 1988. Dad Nelson died the next winter following a fall, which resulted in a fractured hip. Complications followed, and when he died we were free from the responsibility as care-givers to elderly parents. We remained in good health and could empathize with Caleb to some degree when he said, "... I am as strong this day as I was in the day that Moses sent me into battle" (Joshua 14:11). Of course, our battle had not been in the Sinai·Desert, but we could possibly equate it with our nearly 40 years in the Philippines with the Navy and then with ABWE.

We were alive and well, and getting restless for the battle. In our case that meant medical mission work. In consulting with our mission leadership, we found listening ears and were assured that if one of the ABWE field councils having a medical unit requested short-term help, we would be encouraged to go. From past experience we knew that every medical team has recurring personnel shortages created by furloughs, medical leaves and other emergencies. We remembered how often we had longed for someone to take our place for a few months in order to recharge our physical, mental and spiritual batteries.

The Association of Baptists for World Evangelism, Inc., has medical units working in five countries of the world. Listed in the order of their opening, they include the Philippines, Bangladesh, Togo, The Gambia (these latter two in West Africa) and Amazonas, Brazil. Within the first five years of "retirement" we had short-term assignments in each of these countries. Since then, we have revisited several of them. Usually such work visits coincide with a career surgeon's furlough or emergency leave. The time of involvement varies from one to three months.

Since all of these hospitals are in the tropics, the types of medical and surgical cases are similar: complicated pregnancies, emergency abdominal conditions such as appendicitis, obstructions, parasitic diseases of all kinds, tuberculosis, typhoid fever and its complications, and eye conditions, to name a representative few.

Usually, a visiting doctor or nurse works alongside a national who is fluent in the regional language(s) as well as in English, so a translator is an essential part of the team. One advantage of working with a translator is that you avoid making some of the blunders on a cultural level. There may be regional taboos or subtle ways of communicating that are not verbal, ways which only a person fluent in the language and culturally oriented notices.

For instance, during our introduction to the southern part of the Philippines, we spent half of each day with a tutor in the language of that area: Cebuano Visayan. Then we practiced what we were learning as we worked with patients at the clinic. I recall asking questions that had simple "yes" or "no" answers. Without my hearing a reply, the translator would give me the patient's response. Finally, I asked how she knew the answer before the patient had responded.

"Oh, but she did respond. She raised her eyebrows!" A negative was a barely perceivable gesture of the head or lips. And pointing directions is done with the lips. As a matter of fact, some are so good at it that they can indicate something that is behind their backs!

To compound the confusion, the body language in one culture may have the opposite meaning in another. In Bangladesh, for instance, there is a very subtle twisting shake of the head indicating an affirmative response. Elsewhere it could be construed as a negative reaction. Furthermore, in Muslim cultures you consider the left hand as unclean and never use it for eating or offering something to someone else. And dress codes are very different, especially for women. The garments are meant to cover the legs completely down to the ankles, while the midriff may have a wide exposure and be fashionable.

Bangladesh was formerly known as East Pakistan. Through a civil war with West Pakistan it became independent in December 1971 with a new name meaning "land of the Bengalis."[1] Bordered on the west, north and part of the east by India and Myanmar (formerly Burma) on the southeast, it is a densely populated country "...marked by coups, counter-coups, martial law, the quick rise and fall of political leaders, unrest, and a general feeling of discontent over the independence the people had fought so dearly to obtain."

Its population of over 130,000,000 is crowded into an area no larger than the state of Wisconsin. Life expectancy of the Bangladeshi hovers around 50 years, with an infant mortality rate of 135 per 1,000

---

[1] *Bangladesh at a Glance*, ABWE Literature Division, Chittagong, Bangladesh, 1980

live births. Its climate is tropical and subject to cyclones and floods. ABWE's medical evangelism was initiated in the city of Chittagong in 1958 by two nurses, Mary Lou Brownell and Juanita Canfield. They first worked out of a small room for about one year, with occasional clinics in villages nearby. In 1963 Dr. Viggo Olsen and nurses Becky Davey and Jeannie Lockerbie reopened the clinic while in language study in that city. Soon other medical colleagues joined the team: Drs. Ketcham and Ankenman; nurse Jean Weld; and medical technologist Bob Adolph. That same year land was obtained at the site chosen as most strategic for a mission hospital: Malumghat, on the southeastern extremity of the country a few miles inland from the Bay of Bengal.

The construction of a 50 bed medical facility, named the *Memorial Christian Hospital*, began in 1964, and the doors opened for the first patients in 1966. Dr. Olsen was the first medical director while Dr. Donn Ketcham took charge of the surgical department. Many ABWE medical personnel have come and gone since then. Problems plagued them at various times, including the necessity of a short period of closure during an epidemic that afflicted its personnel. Nevertheless, the Lord has continued to bless its ministry to a population area of over ten million needy people, 85% of whom are Muslims and 14% Hindus. Language and cultural barriers are quite a challenge, especially for the short-term doctor or nurse, such as we.

In West Africa, too, we found that translators are invaluable. Take Gaglo, for instance. He is an African, beloved of the Lord, without whom I would have been severely handicapped in the out-patient clinic of the *Karolyn Kempton Memorial Christian Hospital* in Togo. I could speak a few phrases in French and muddle along, but most patients spoke a regional language: Ewe, Kabye, or one of several others. Gaglo always understood them and told me what the problem was.

I intentionally specified his value in the *clinic* work because Gaglo wasn't needed in the operating room. In that setting, I didn't have to converse with the patient. He or she was anesthetized and I was there to repair the hernia or remove the tumor or do whatever was needed. My technical assistants (Kossi, Etienne, or Bawa) knew the instruments whether I called for them in English or French, or just pointed to the specific piece needed at the time. We didn't talk much at the operating table. Besides, Lenore was usually the circulating nurse and she understood me well. We could communicate freely as she kept track of the vital signs and general condition of the patient. She kept us supplied with the right sutures and other supplies as needed. As time went on during our stay, the technicians became more and more proficient in English, and we picked up a few Togolese words.

Of course, a few tense moments are inevitable in surgery. As one anesthesiologist analyzed his work: "It consists of long periods of boredom, punctuated by short bursts of panic." I knew what he meant when we were performing surgery on Bruce Ebersole, one of our missionary kids. His father, in gown and mask, was with him in the operating room, which is not an uncommon practice in a mission hospital. I administered the spinal anesthetic, turned Bruce over and began the hernia repair. About fifteen minutes into the procedure, the nurse at the head of the table announced in a concerned voice, "Bruce isn't breathing."

That emergency took priority over the open wound. I asked my assistant, Dr. Rene Sison, to continue while I broke scrub and went to the head of the table. Indeed, Bruce was paralyzed below his neck. Furthermore, his lips were getting a bit dusky. I knew immediately that the anesthetic had risen higher than intended, numbing the nerves that control the breathing muscles of the diaphragm and chest. That is a rather rare reaction which we had encountered before. So I began mouth-to-mouth resuscitation while the nurse hooked up the oxygen line and got the respirator working.

You can well imagine what was going through the mind of Russ, Bruce's father. We tried to reassure him and sent him out for a few minutes to restore his own breathing. Bruce was back on his own within a few minutes and I could change my wet gown for a fresh one and pull on a pair of new gloves. By that time, Dr. Sison had proceeded with the surgery to the point where I had only to add a few finishing touches and close the wound. Bruce's recovery was uneventfully smooth after that.

To this day, both Bruce and his father vividly recall what they would describe as "panic time." A comment by one of our mission pilots described a similar feeling of anxiety that may occur while flying. He insisted that the propeller on the single engine planes he flew, was really just a big fan. Said he, "If you don't believe it, just see how the pilot sweats if it stops while he's in the air!"

I must confess that having an anesthetist or an anesthesiologist at the head end of the operating table makes the surgeon much more relaxed as he does his work. Yet the average small mission hospital does not have the "luxury" of a person who is trained in that department. Consequently, the surgeon is in charge of both the anesthesia and the procedure. Therefore, some of the major types of surgery such as heart, lung and brain must be transferred by air-lift or other means to a city that has those capabilities.

Have you ever thought about how many specially talented people make up a missionary enterprise? There are pastors, teachers, and evangelists to be sure. But there are also the linguists involved in translating the scriptures, literacy specialists teaching people how to read the Bible after it is translated, medical professionals, engineers and mechanics who keep the machinery running, bookkeepers and administrators. The list could go on. Positions are even open for retirees to manage missionary guest facilities or to supervise missionary school children as dormitory parents. Yes, these are all *missionaries* in every sense of the word, sharing the workload in a variety of ways.

In Luke 5:17-26 we read the amazing story of the healing of a man who was totally paralyzed. Jesus was teaching in a village, and a crowd gathered where He was staying. Four unnamed friends of the paralytic carried him to the house in order that Jesus would heal him. They knew Jesus could do it! They ran into a problem, however. The crowds were so insensitive that they completely blocked the entrance. But that didn't deter the four litter-bearers from their goal. They carried the man on his straw mat up the outside stairway to

WITH SCALPEL AND THE SWORD

the roof of the house. Then, they tore up the roof right over the area where Jesus was teaching. Imagine the scene: the obvious distraction of their removing the tiles and the inevitable spillage of roofing fragments down to those underneath. But that didn't stop them. They made a hole large enough to lower their friend on his mat right at the feet of Jesus. They must have used ropes tied to each corner of their improvised stretcher. Then, seeing *their* faith, Jesus made this remarkable statement: "Man, thy sins are forgiven thee ... Arise, take up thy couch, and go into thine house" (Luke 5:20, 23).

Those four burden-bearers were remarkable in several ways: first, they are *anonymous*, just ordinary men. Second, they had an unusual concern for their friend; they were *compassionate*. Third, they had an uncommon *faith* in the power of Jesus of Nazareth. Fourth, they were *driven* by determination to accomplish their goal. Fifth, they were *innovative* making a unique way to Jesus. Finally, *they didn't consider the cost* in sweat, tears and money (who do you think paid for repairing the roof?).

I don't know of a better illustration of qualities that missionaries ought to possess: compassion, motivation, determination, innovation, sacrifice — all for the glory of God and the eternal salvation of the hopeless. God give us more men and women who are willing to *spend and be spent* ... **weary, perhaps, yet pursuing!**

APPENDIX

DEVELOPMENT OF THE FUNDAMENTAL BAPTIST MOVEMENT IN MINDANAO, PHILIPPINES

A. ABWE PERSONNEL ASSIGNMENTS in the 1950's-1980's:

HENRY & GLADYS DeVRIES and RHODA LITTLE joined ABWE in 1938, transferring from another mission under which they had come to Mindanao. They worked as a team in Mindanao, establishing their first church in Malaybalay, plus several others in outlying villages. They were known throughout the province, both in the lowland and in the mountains. Since she was a nurse, Rhoda trekked the trails and lovingly brought medical help along with the gospel message. Providentially, she was on furlough when the Japanese invaded Mindanao in World War II, but the DeVries family was captured and interned in Japanese prison camps for over three years. Henry, Gladys and Rhoda returned for another term after the war.

BOB & GRACE KOHLER and LOUISE LYNIP are grouped together since they lived and worked as a team on the far side of the backbone of mountains that runs down the middle of Bukidnon. They served many years in Bukidnon prior to World War II, and were among the few ABWE missionaries to successfully elude the Japanese occupation forces. In late 1943 or early in 1944, after months of hiding in the mountains of Mindanao, they were rescued by American sailors on the northern coast of Mindanao and spirited away on American submarines to Australia. They returned to the Philippines in 1945 where Louise established Bethany Home, an orphanage in the town of Talakag. The Kohlers concentrated on church planting in that same area, where they continue to live in retirement.

REV. & MRS. WILLIAM GOLDIE arrived in Bukidnon shortly after World War II, and worked alongside the family of Henry DeVries until early 1952. Rev. Goldie eventually returned to duty with the U.S. Army as a chaplain.

ALFRED & RUTH CONANT arrived in Bukidnon around 1950 under. Alfred became the pastor of Bethel Baptist Church in Malaybalay and served in that capacity until the latter part of 1952. The Conant family moved to Davao province to begin a new ABWE ministry in Tagum. Other ministry opportunities opened for them in Iloilo City and Baguio City prior to retirement.

HUMBERT & JEANNE TENTARELLI began church planting together in Bukidnon in 1949. Jeanne (nee Wagner) worked alongside Rhoda Little for one term immediately after the War in 1945. Both were nurses, and they established a small dispensary on the site of the present Bethel Baptist Hospital. After they married, Humbert and Jeanne concentrated on developing churches in the northern sector of Bukidnon, moving their residence to Tankulan (later to be renamed Manolo Fortich) in 1953. They also were instrumental in planting churches in the province of Misamis Oriental, on the northern border of Bukidnon. They retired in 1969.

RON & LAURA ("DAVIE") ESSON arrived in Bukidnon in the fall of 1951. Ron was a pharmacist and Davie a nurse. They assumed responsibility for the medical work at Bethel Baptist Clinic. I have recorded their exploits over the subsequent 25 years in the main text.

PRISCILLA BAILEY and MILDRED CROUCH ("the Aunties") came to Bukidnon in December of 1951. Their expertise with children and young people endeared them to many. Early on, they took over the dormitory for Bukidnon girls attending high school in Malaybalay. They taught in the short-term Bible Institutes, developed Sunday School materials, and assisted church planters in opening new churches and new fields. In their third term of service, they joined the ABWE team in southern Leyte. The Aunties wound up their missionary careers managing the ABWE guest houses (Doane Rest) in Baguio City.

LINK & LENORE NELSON arrived in April 1952. The Nelsons spent 25 years in Malaybalay, during which they saw the construction of two additional wings of the hospital. In 1977 they moved to the new mission hospital in Hilongos, Leyte, where they worked for ten more years before retiring in 1988. They tell their story in this autobiography.

ORLAN & MABEL WILHITE arrived in late1954 to participate in church planting in Bukidnon for their first four-year term. They transferred later to Baguio City and opened a youth center there, attracting many to Bible studies and affiliation with the regional Baptist church fellowship. Health problems forced the Wilhites into early retirement.

EARL AND PHYLLIS CARLBERG joined the Bukidnon team in 1955, taking up residence in Tankulan when the Tentarellies left on furlough. Earl became a tireless church planter. They later moved their residence to Malaybalay which enabled Phyllis, a certified school teacher, to help start Bethel Baptist Academy (BBA) in the summer of 1957.

ELLA GROVER arrived in Malaybalay in 1957 to set up the clinical laboratory in Bethel Baptist Hospital. When the Essons left for furlough, she took on the added tasks of business manager. In 1978 she transferred to the Palawan Baptist Hospital to set up their laboratory and business departments. She faithfully served there until her retirement in 1989.

ROSEMARY ULLERY was appointed by ABWE in 1954 and she spent the next ten years in the Philippines. She divided her time between Davao and Bukidnon, where she worked in the newly constructed infirmary wing of Bethel Baptist Hospital as a licensed vocational nurse (LVN). She was also involved in personal evangelism, and assisted in children and youth ministries.

CATHERINE (KAY) MOLLOHAN, DORIS WARD and ALMA SHOEMAKER also joined the Bukidnon team in the mid-1950's: Kay as a nurse on the hospital staff; and Alma and Doris as youth workers and Christian education leaders.

DAVID & BEULAH SHERIDAN became involved in Bethel Baptist Academy when they arrived for the 1958-59 school year. Their first assignment was as dormitory parents for the boarding children who came from other areas of the southern Philippines. Dave also taught classes in the academy and became the principal when the Carlbergs left for furlough. Beulah's expertise was in the arts department. They ministered with the Davao ABWE team during their second term beginning in 1965. Health problem shortened their career, causing them to take an early retirement from the mission in 1975.

HEDWIG ("HEDIE") HELSTEN also joined the BBA faculty in the school year 1958-59. When she was first appointed by ABWE in 1948, she was scheduled to go to China. But when that field closed due to the Communist take-over, she was reassigned to Iloilo, Philippines, arriving in 1950. She taught in Doane Baptist Bible Institute until 1958 when she transferred to Malaybalay to teach at the academy. Hedie had to return to the USA on sick leave the fall of 1960, could not return to the field, and eventually retired from ABWE.

EVELYN MORGAN left the USA for her first term with ABWE in early 1961. She taught in the Bethel Baptist Academy until it was eventually closed some years later. Then she transferred to the faculty of Faith Academy in Manila.

BOB & GRACE BEIKERT were appointed by ABWE in 1962. In 1964 they worked briefly as dormitory parents to MK's attending Bethel Baptist Academy in Malaybalay. Bob was gifted in the area of management. Because of an urgent need for his expertise, the family moved to Manila where Bob became manager of the ABWE business office.

HELEN MILLER moved to Malaybalay with her four children in 1963. She had served with her husband Paul in India on the border of Tibet in 1947, translating the scriptures and being involved in personal evangelism. They transferred to East Pakistan (later to be renamed Bangladesh) in 1957 to join the newly formed ABWE team. But Paul became critically ill with poliomyelitis and died in Chittagong in May of 1959. Helen, Paul's widow, applied to help fill the need for a dormitory parent and also teach MK's in Bethel Baptist Academy (BBA).

RAYDENE TAYLOR came on the scene in late 1964 to teach at BBA in Malaybalay until the school was phased out. She then assisted full-time with the church planting team in Davao province where she concentrated on preparing TEE materials, youth projects, and later organized the AWANA program for the entire Philippines (AFBCP).

CLINTON & DOROTHY BONNELL were appointed for the field of Davao and arrived in the Philippines March 1957. After language study in Cebu City, Clint & Dotty went to Davao to join the ABWE church planters, joining Dee Taylor in Tagum. Their second term involved work in Faith Academy in Manila where Clint taught and Dotty served as school nurse in the infirmary. They also filled in as dorm parents.

FRANK AND NANCY HARTWIG joined the Davao ABWE team

after completing their language requirements in Manila in 1967. They quickly adapted to their new environment and were very effective in church planting work.

BILL & MARILYN STEVENSON became an integral part of the medical team at Bethel Baptist Hospital in 1970. Bill preceded Marilyn to the Philippines as a widower, having lost his first wife to cancer in 1966. Marilyn joined him in Malaybalay where they were married on the hospital compound October 24, 1970. They helped open the Leyte Baptist Clinic during their second term in 1975 and were active in church planting with the ABWE team there.

DAVID & SUSAN BLACK found their way to Mindanao in 1974. David's special interest was in Christian Education, especially Theological Education by Extension (TEE). They teamed up with Raydene Taylor in Davao province. They later transferred to southern Leyte to teach TEE for a year before finishing their term in the Manila Baptist Church.

LARRY & THELMA HOLMAN entered the ABWE aviation ministry in 1975 and came to help in Malaybalay with their family. Larry was a former military pilot with many flight hours. He was involved in opening the ABWE aviation ministry in Bukidnon. They transferred to the province of Palawan in the latter part of 1976 to start another flying program at the Palawan Baptist Hospital in the town of Roxas.

DAVID & BECKY NELSON arrived in Malaybalay with their two boys, Jeff and Josh, to take over the aviation ministry in Bukidnon in February 1977. They had completed their initial language study in Cebu City prior to this. They took up residence next door to Dave's parents on the hospital compound and became involved in both flying and church planting ministries for two terms. They then transferred to southern Leyte for another term. After the aviation department was phased out, Dave became the Coordinator for ABWE Philippines and moved to the Manila area until their resignation for health reasons in 1993.

DON & BARBARA LOVE brought their expertise as medical technologist and nurse, respectively, to help in the building and development of the mission hospitals in Leyte and Aklan. They were appointed to work with ABWE in August 1971 and arrived in the Philippines in June 1973. After basic orientation and language study in Manila, they moved down to Hilongos, Leyte in June 1974 to develop the laboratory of Leyte Baptist Clinic. They were both on the staff there until requested to help in the development of the new facility in Aklan in September of 1982. They moved from Aklan to Manila in May 1985 to manage the ABWE office. In 1989 they Loves left the field in order to meet family needs in the USA.

BERNIE & CAROLE BEVERLY were appointed to Bukidnon in 1976 to be a second pilot on the team in Malaybalay; however, they discovered that the greater need was in church planting work. They transferred to Davao province and put their full time into that ministry. They helped establish at least two local Baptist Churches before Bernie's election to the office of the ABWE Field Coordinator, necessitating their moveto Manila in the early 1980's.

KEN & ALICE COLE joined the medical team in Leyte about 1979. Several years earlier, Ken had visited the ABWE hospital in Malaybalay as a medical student on a three-month rotation from medical school. About that same time, Alice Augsburger was appointed by ABWE to the Hong Kong field and was engrossed in language study. In God's perfect way and timing, they met and married. Ken's medical degree suited them to accept an invitation to join the medical group in Hilongos, Leyte. Later the Coles settled into a church-planting ministry in the Manila area. Ken served several terms as ABWE Field Coordinator.

JIM & ESTHER ENTNER joined the ABWE medical team in

Palawan in 1971 and were on hand when the new hospital opened in Roxas in 1977. Esther's expertise was with youth work in the regional Baptist fellowship of churches. Later they became involved in both the Mindanao and the Leyte hospitals as staff shortages required their help. As these units became autonomous, the Entners took on an advisory role and eventually concentrated on the church-planting work in Cebu City together with the Klumpps.

THE LARRY ARMSTRONGS, JIM ANKENYS, DE PAYTONS and PHIL KLUMPPS constituted the church-planters on Leyte during the developing years of that new work in the 1970's and 1980's. Their church planters worked alongside their Filipino colleagues and the medical team. The joint effort resulted in the opening of many churches in that province. Although not Mindanao missionaries, they must be included for completeness.

B. THE BUKIDNON ASSOCIATION OF BAPTIST CHURCHES (BABC)

In the years prior to the 1950's, there were fewer than twenty local churches in the Bukidnon fellowship. In 1951 the decision was made to form the Association known as the BABC. The purpose was to unite the local churches in fellowship and goals through annual conference meetings and cooperative work on Association projects.

Although I do not have a record of the original officers of the council of the BABC, a brochure of their 25th annual conference held in April of 1976 lists the council members at their Silver Jubilee as Rev. Ernesto Rivera, Rev. Norberto Selorio, Pastor V. Decena, Pastor M. Alinob, Mr. A. Aston, and Dr. Lincoln Nelson. Rev. Nestor Gapulan was then the regional evangelist.

By the year 1976 there were 76 churches listed in the BABC. The association was subdivided into four sectors: northern, central, southern and mountain. That promoted closer regional cooperation in church planting, in the production of Christian literature for Sunday schools, and in providing an on-going theological education for pastors and lay-leaders.

C. EXISTING FELLOWSHIP BAPTIST CHURCHES IN BUKIDNON IN THE EARLY 1950's

Churches in Bukidnon	Date of Constitution
1. Bethel Baptist Church, Malaybalay: Rev. Antonio Ormeo	1953

Note: Organized with officers about 1930, but with constitution in 1953

2. Berean Baptist Church, Casisang: Rev. N. Industan	1931
3. Emmanuel Baptist Church, Manalog: Mr. Guinano	1937
4. Bugcaon Baptist Church, Bugcaon: Mr. Gonlivo	1937
5. United Baptist Church, Laguitas: Pastor Dumala	1940
6. Maramag Baptist Church: Pastor Sinagda	1947
7. Valencia Baptist Church: Rev. Norberto Selorio	1947
8. Canayan Baptist Church: Mr. Santiago	1948
9. Faith Baptist Church, Cabanglasan: Mr. Sayusay	1949
10. Redeemed Baptist Ch., Bontongon: Mr. Pinohon	1952
11. Faith Baptist Ch, Caburacanan: Mr. Monsamay	1952
12. Grace Baptist Ch, Kalasungay:	1952

Rev. Lumilang
13. Kibawe Baptist Church: 1953
    Pastor M.Hindrana
14. Trinity Baptist Church, Lambagan: 1953
    Mr. Siblian
15. Pinamaloy Baptist Church: 1953
    Pastor Sorita
16. Glory Baptist Church, Kibalabag: 1953
    Mr. Aud
17. Rapture Baptist Church, Patpat: 1953
    Mr. Daglinao
18. Salvation Bpt. Ch, Old Cabanglasan: 1953
    Mr.Andapat
19. Lonocan Baptist Church: 1953
    Mr. Nunez
20. Tankulan Baptist Church: 1953
    Rev. Humbert Tentarelli

The total number of baptized members in these local churches in Bukidnon is given as 1,001 in 1953. It is of interest that in 1953, eight churches were added that had been organized much earlier, and presumably had regional official status. However, each lacked a local church constitution prior to 1953.

A similar record of Fellowship Baptist churches in **Davao** province prior to 1952 has not been found. However, the churches or groups that invited Rev. Conant and the evangelistic team in 1952 were located in Tagum, Compostela, Mawab, Panabo and Pagsabangan.

D. SHORT-TERM BIBLE INSTITUTES IN BUKIDNON

One of the most important ministries of the ABWE missionaries in the 1950's was that of teaching in what were known as "Short-Term Bible Institutes." Those were regular gatherings of the pastors and workers of the province in a host church. They began as two-week seminars held on a quarterly basis. As time went on, the frequency changed to thrice a year, then twice a year, and finally gave way to the establishing of a regional Bible Institute with full time faculty and organized curriculum. In this way the growing number of churches had a supply of trained graduates from which to call pastors.

The participants chose the host church by a poll at the end of each session, rotating the venue among the 20 or so churches. Friendly and enthusiastic rivalry filled the atmosphere as churches vied for the privilege of being the site of the next Institute. The institutes benefitted the local host church greatly. The attraction of out-of-town visitors added prestige to the church in the eyes of the community. The evening services were always open to the public and the evangelistic theme reached the hearts of unsaved neighbors, aiding church growth.

It didn't seem to matter how distant the host church might be. Sometimes the conferees rode for hours on a bus, crossed rivers and hiked through muddy trails, and traversed mountains just to get there. The regional ABWE missionaries composed the faculty, together with an occasional guest speaker/lecturer. The institutes rated high priority; even the clinic staff participated, though that required shutting down some of the medical activity for a short time. (A skeleton staff was left to take care of emergencies.)

The result, however, proved the importance of the seminars. Many pastors and workers, who had not been privileged to attend an organized Bible institute or college, were given significant training to better equip them for the vital task of leading their flock. Faithful students who completed the courses accumulated credits so that official recognition could be given to the graduates.

E. THE MINDANAO BAPTIST BIBLE INSTITUTE (MBBI)

After several years, the short-term Bible institutes were phased out. In their place the Bukidnon Association of Baptist Churches' conferees voted to establish a regional Bible School, at the recommendation of their council. Experience had taught them that many provincial students who went to the city for Bible training often failed to return to pastor churches in their home province. They reasoned that the best solution would be to have their own Bible school in Bukidnon.

In 1956 Pastor Antonio Ormeo, Rev. Earl Carlberg and Alma Shoemaker became the faculty for the first classes. The venue was the Bethel Baptist Church in Malaybalay which was located on the ABWE mission compound at that time. At first it was named The Baptist Workers Training Institute (BWTI). In 1961-62 the school moved into new facilities built on the property of the Valencia Baptist Church. At that time the name of the school was changed to Mindanao Baptist Bible Institute (MBBI) which finally moved to property between Valencia and Malaybalay at Nasuli, Bukidnon. A Christian landowner there donated the property immediately adjacent to the compound of the Summer Institute of Linguistics (SIL), a branch of Wycliffe Bible Translators.

Through the years the board members and teachers of MBBI included such capable members as Rev. Norberto Selorio, Rev. Ernesto Rivera, Rev. Naparete Dulag, Rev. and Mrs. Severino Basa, Rev. Rudy Escobar, Rev. Eduardo Lumilang, Rev. Tony Kangleon and Rev. Nestor Gapulan. The Wycliffe Translators at Nasuli have been very supportive of the school in many ways. It continues to be supported and maintained by its independent board of directors, backed by the regional Baptist Churches.

F. THE ASSOCIATION OF BAPTISTS FOR PHILIPPINE EVANGELISM, INC. (ABPE)

The conferees at the Bukidnon short-term institute in 1963 expressed their burden for the island of Bohol. Their concern resulted in the formation of The Bukidnon Association of Baptists for Philippine Evangelism, Inc. (BABPE), organized in October 1964. The goal of this organization was to send Filipino missionaries to "home-mission" projects. These missionaries would be supported by the Bukidnon churches. Their first field would be the island of Bohol. As the BABPE considered other outreaches beyond their association's borders, the entire Association of Fundamental Baptist Churches in the Philippines became interested in a country-wide cooperative program. So the organization was renamed The Association of Baptists for Philippine Evangelism (ABPE).

Humbert Tentarelli reported in January of 1966 that of the several young people who were challenged to join this newly organized agency, the first to qualify was a young lady named Erminda Perez. She was a graduate of Doane Baptist Bible Institute in Iloilo City, and was burdened for Bohol where her father had been born. Her support was promised and she sailed on the ship "*MV SWEET HOPE*" arriving in Bohol exactly three years to the day that the home mission project was organized.

It wasn't long before others applied to work in Bohol and were found qualified. Among them were Rev. & Mrs. Sixto Medel, Rev. & Mrs. Pablito Ga-as, Rev. & Mrs. Gequillana, Rev. & Mrs. Agripino Baldimor applied for the field of Camiguin and were accepted.

The members of the ABPE Board of Directors from 1976-1981 were listed on the brochure of the 25th Annual Conference of the BABC: Rev. Ernesto Rivera, President; Rev. Rudy Escobar, Vice

President; Rev. Severino Basa, Secretary; Rev. Nestor Gapulan, Treasurer; Rev. Lucilo Rafols, Auditor & Davao Representative; and Rev. Norberto Selorio, Rev. Ben Asinero and Rev. Adriano Sinohon were members.

G. THE FUNDAMENTAL BAPTIST MISSION

Another interesting home-missions project developed later. The Association of Fundamental Baptist Churches in the Philippines (AFBCP) had observed the lack of a strong fundamental Baptist testimony on Luzon's Bicol peninsula. This became a personal obsession with Pastor Rudy Escobar (a member of the Board of the ABPE). Though an effective and beloved pastor of the Maramag Baptist Church in Bukidnon at the time, he resigned to enter an independent faith ministry, the Fundamental Baptist Mission in the mid 1980's.

The Escobar family moved first to Camiguin to spearhead a Baptist testimony there. Later when the Baldimors were able to take over that ministry, the Escobars moved to the Bicol area. Norma, pastor Escobar's wife, was also able to get a position as teacher in an elementary school in the city. The Escobars organized a sound church whose members built a beautiful Baptist church building at a great cost, from the human viewpoint. One of the first services conducted in the new building was Norma's funeral. She had been stricken with a severe attack of asthma from which she never recovered. The only cemetery in that city was closed to non-Catholics. So the ABWE pilot air-lifted her body to the town of her birth.

About two months after this seeming tragedy, Pastor Escobar wrote: "Norma's death was so sudden that it took me this long to write. Humanly speaking, I still tremble to recall in writing what took place that night of February 25, 1984. Since that day when the Lord took my beloved wife, every waking hour I pray for strength and courage to accept God's plan and thank Him for everything. He gave me victory over my mental and emotional anguish. I knew 'We are more than conquerors through Him that loves us.' ... For the first time in my life I can say without hypocrisy ...

Thank you Lord for the trials that come my way.
In that way I can grow each day, as I let you lead.
I thank you Lord for the patience that trials bring,
in that process of growing I can learn to care.

But it goes against the way I am, to put my human nature down
and let the Spirit take control of all I do,
'Cause when those trials come,
My human nature shouts the thing to do
And God's soft prompting can be easily ignored.

Thank you Lord for the victory that growing brings,
In surrender of everything life is so worthwhile,
And I thank you Lord that when everything's put in place,
Out in front I can see your face and it's there you belong."
(*THANK YOU LORD*, by Dan Burgess)

(signed) Pastor Escobar & children
Balm, Flobie, Rubie, Zion and Shalom

H. THE ASSOCIATION OF FUNDAMENTAL BAPTIST CHURCHES IN THE PHILIPPINES (AFBCP)

As early as 1952 it became apparent that there was the need for a nationwide association of the Fundamental Baptist movement. The goal was to coordinate the evangelistic outreach of those churches, both at home and abroad. Six regional councils made up the association: Northern Luzon, Southern Luzon & Palawan, Western Visayan, Eastern Visayan, Northern Mindanao and Southern Mindanao. They named the organization the Association of Fundamental Baptist Churches in the Philippines (AFBCP). It met biennially with an effort to rotate the venues to these six regions according to the majority choice of the messengers in session.

The council of the AFBCP was comprised of the chairmen of the six regions, plus representatives from the two Bible Institutes: Baptist Bible Institute and Seminary in the Greater Manila area; and Doane Baptist Bible Institute in Iloilo City. The council invited two ABWE missionaries to join the council meetings as consultants.

This national body conceived the formation of a mission agency to facilitate the international outreach of the Philippine churches. In the biennial meeting in 1964 in the city of Tagum, Davao, the Philippine Association of Baptists for World Evangelism (PABWE) was born. The AFBCP council appointed a survey team to search out the target country for the first foreign mission project. The team studied and visited several nations in Southeast Asia, and recommended to the AFBCP in its next session that they should enter the field of Thailand.

I. THE PHILIPPINE ASSOCIATION OF BAPTISTS FOR WORLD EVANGELISM, INC. (PABWE)

One of the pastors from Davao, Rev. Roberto Gequillana, was a member of the team which surveyed Thailand. He was among the first to apply to be one of the missionaries to that country. Supporting AFBCP churches promised their financial and prayer backing. Soon he and his wife Barbara were on their way to Bangkok. The first single woman missionary appointed by the PABWE Board was Lourdes Jardenico. She was able to raise her support after several months of deputation among the AFBCP churches. In 1967 she flew to join the team in Bangkok. The other missionaries in that early group were Rev. & Mrs. Richfield Cudal, Rev. & Mrs. Delfin Ecate, Rev. & Mrs. Arturo Inion, and another single woman, Miss Cagas. From time to time other candidates were appointed, including Rev. Pete and Melody Wong.

Several facts need to be high-lighted about PABWE and its missionaries. Foremost is the fact that the mission was and continues to be the autonomous project of the Filipino churches, both in personnel and in finances. This points up the truth that foreign mission work is not the exclusive domain of western nations. As an Asian conference speaker wisely stated: "God did not set up His mission headquarters in America!" Christ's commission was first to the believers in Asia — and the middle east in particular (Matthew 28:18-20).

Secondly, the "track-record" has shown that Filipinos are uniquely able to reach Asians with the gospel. They are quick to learn difficult foreign languages and adapt readily to living conditions in a different culture. They far out-strip the ability of expatriates from western countries. Americans are amazed when they observe Filipino missionaries in Thailand open a Bible School and teach new converts in the Thai language within their first term in that country.

And thirdly, nothing stimulates growth of local churches more than sending out their own missionaries. Whereas there were only 20 churches in Bukidnon province in 1950, in 1990 that one province had over 200 Fundamental Baptist Churches.

An interesting side-light on the life of that first woman missionary, Lourdes: she is now Mrs. Charles Holmes, married to an energetic American missionary. Together they continue to serve the Lord in Thailand. They met in Bangkok where he was engaged in a business enterprise, but now he is putting his full time into church planting ministries as they work alongside the PABWE team of missionaries.

J. THE MINDORO MEDICAL OUTREACH

Although most of this book deals with anecdotes from our experience in three of the mission hospitals in the Philippines which we helped start, the tale of another hospital located on the island of Mindoro is worth mentioning for the record.

In 1968 a young doctor, named Romeo Santiago, had recently graduated from medical college and asked to join the staff of Bethel Baptist Hospital. Romeo came from the Manila area and was an alert, enthusiastic young Christian. He wanted to gain experience in developing a small mission hospital like BBH. He had been requested by the Guadalupe Baptist Church in Metro Manila to become the physician for its Mindoro medical outreach at the chosen site for the outreach in Maluanluan in the province of Oriental Mindoro.

He worked faithfully for about a year at Bethel and was quick to learn the basic surgical procedures. When the *Mindoro Medical Outreach* was officially inaugurated on January 19, 1969, Dr. Santiago was introduced to the crowd attending the ceremony in Maluanluan as the director of that medical facility. Along with the pastor of Guadalupe Baptist Church, Rev. Jose Galuego, were other dignitaries: the *barrio* captain, several town councilors, prominent families of that village, Pastor Zacarias Cometa of the nearby Makati Baptist Church, and evangelist Pedro Angkahan. Dr. Bill Stevenson attended as the ABWE representative.

Also attending were Rev. and Mrs. Rudolpho Agapito, recent graduates of Baptist Bible Seminary and Institute in Taytay, Rizal. They became the hospital evangelists when the medical unit opened. Before long, *Grace Baptist Hospital* was a reality. In its first year, Dr. Angelita Corpuz joined the staff. ABWE personnel continued to keep in touch and helped whenever possible. While in Manila for language study, Drs. Jim Entner and Bill Stevenson each made occasional work-visits to encourage Dr. Santiago and his clinic workers.

The first anniversary of the hospital was celebrated with a weekend of special meetings. On hand were the Kintners, Beikerts, Dave Boehning and Jim Enter to congratulate and support the Grace Baptist Hospital staff and its officers.

As time went on, the hospital was enlarged to about one hundred beds. It also became a nurses-training facility. God used Dr. Santiago and his staff to effectively reach that area with the gospel of Christ. *Grace Baptist Hospital* is highly respected in the community. And Bethel Baptist Hospital was privileged to have a part in the fulfillment of the vision of Guadalupe Baptist Church.

K. THE ABWE/AFBCP MEDICAL FACILITIES

The following is a list of mission hospitals started by ABWE personnel in the Philippines in the order of their development. Details will be left out, since much of the narratives appear in the body of this work.

1. BETHEL BAPTIST HOSPITAL, Malaybalay, Bukidnon,1955.
2. LEYTE BAPTIST CLINIC & HOSPITAL, Hilongos, Leyte,1975.
3. PALAWAN BAPTIST HOSPITAL, Roxas, Palawan,1977.
4. AKLAN BAPTIST HOSPITAL, Caticlan, Malay, Aklan, 1982.

PALAWAN BAPTIST HOSPITAL (PBH)

Although this is primarily a book about the author's involvement in Mindanao plus a reference to the expansion to both Leyte and Aklan, I do not wish to imply that the Palawan Baptist Hospital is of lesser importance. On the contrary, it supplies a vital service to the northern half of those "shoe-string" islands of Palawan on the extreme western side of the Philippines. A brief history of its founding is included here.

In February of 1964, Ron Esson was asked to participate in a survey with members of ABWE's Palawan Field Council to determine the feasibility of another medical-missions project locating there. Mr. & Mrs. Bud DeVries, Rev. Frank Morse, and Mr. & Mrs. Ron Esson constituted the ABWE survey team. Irv Allan was the pilot of the Mission Aviation Fellowship plane that flew them at times, and Pastor Haberadas, chief engineer of the gospel launch, went along when the team travelled by sea. The survey group concluded that Palawan was the right place for a medical team and for the base of a mission plane.

The Essons, therefore, transferred to Palawan in 1966 and started fly-in clinics in 1967 with the services of MAF personnel. The work grew and church development was stimulated. Soon the first missionary physician, Dr. Jim Entner, and his wife Esther completed their study of Tagalog in Manila and joined the Palawan team. Later a second ABWE physician and his wife, Dr. & Mrs. Phil Young, arrived to join them until ill health forced their early resignation. By the mid-1970's it became evident that the field council should make plans to build a mission hospital in the northern section of Palawan at Roxas, about 60 miles (100 kilometers) north of the capital city of Puerto Princesa.

Bud DeVries and a crew of men labored faithfully until a two-story structure was completed in June of 1977 and Palawan Baptist Hospital was dedicated. By that time Dan and Maryanna Horton, both nurses, came to give their invaluable service. Soon a staff of ABWE and national workers had formed. The hospital continues to serve this remote part of the Philippines with the goal of eventually becoming a completely autonomous Filipino ministry, along with the other three mission hospitals listed.